The Elephant in the Room

From Pregnancy to the First Year of Parenthood

Krizia Guerra-Coleman

authorHOUSE®

AuthorHouse™
1663 Liberty Drive
Bloomington, IN 47403
www.authorhouse.com
Phone: 1-800-839-8640

Published by AuthorHouse 01/21/2015

ISBN: 978-1-4969-6258-4 (sc)
ISBN: 978-1-4969-6257-7 (e)

Library of Congress Control Number: 2015900058

Acknowledgements

I want to thank God first of all for the wonderful gift he has given me, my son. Though I did not think it so wonderful at the time it has been the biggest blessing and gift I have ever received in my life. A gift that has changed my life completely to something totally unexpected. God has given me the strength to be able to handle this life change and make it powerful so much so that my entire career has turned to reach out and help others. Without you God I would not be here today and neither would my son. Thank you!

To my husband for supporting me through this process of becoming a mother including the good and the bad times. Especially for supporting me while I wrote this book and encouraging me to touch the lives of other women by educating them on the truth about motherhood.

A special and most grateful thank you to my baby boy. Without you this part of my life would never have happened and I would not be where I am today. Thank you for all that you have taught me of myself, being a parent and loving so profoundly more than I ever thought possible. Because of you this is real. Thank you for changing my life all for the better. I work daily to be the best Mom I can be for you.

Thank you to my therapist that has helped me and guided me through this difficult transition from being a single woman to the best mother I can be. I do not think I would have survived without you. Thank you for your tips and advice you have shared with me. Thank you!

To the mom's at my stroller strides work out class, Thank you for all the support, help, ideas and tips you have passed on to me. Other moms of the world will be grateful to you for sharing your knowledge and experiences.

Contents

Prefix

This book is dedicated to all the women thinking of becoming pregnant, that are pregnant and expecting their first baby, for those women on their second child or more that feel emotionally different from all the stereotypes of what people say "you should feel during pregnancy and as a mom". After starting this book I have also wanted to dedicate this book to woman that have been raped and are pregnant due to that, the woman who have had one night stands, women that are in a relationship and end up pregnant as well as all the young ladies in high school and up that want to be a young mom or that are practicing unsafe sex. I would like this book to be passed on to them so they know what they are really getting themselves into. Being a young mom is not all that you think it would be. Reading this book may just give you a reality check on what parenting is all about and hopefully open your eyes to other things in your own life while developing and getting to know yourself before bringing a new life into this world.

The reason behind this is well, because I wish I would have known or someone would have told me about certain things or "secrets" that are not spoken about when you become pregnant, a mom for the first time or if you remember your experience either with your first pregnancy or with your multiple pregnancies. I touch on some emotions that are O.K. to feel or not to feel during pregnancy or as a mom.

I also mention situations or issues that happen to you that no one talks about during this time. Because it is said to be "taboo" or you are looked down upon as a "bad mother" for feeling this way. This is not true.

I am a Mother. I'm a mom that went to school to be an artist/ teacher and developed a new idea when my baby arrived. I wanted to share with the other moms and moms to be, what I went through and what I have learned. I want other women to know what to really expect or understand what they are feeling and going through. It is O.K. to feel as well as be prepared for what is to come. I'm writing this down to share with other women so we don't "forget" due to sleep deprivation. Giving knowledge so that women are aware of what really happens in pregnancy and beyond and are not taken by surprise because people don't talk about it, things that you regret when you're already pregnant or feel shame for what you feel or don't feel. This is to educate women on the experience called pregnancy and being a mom.

This is not a "what to expect when you're expecting" kind of book... that one is already done. This book is more psychological and some physical aspects, that the other books missed out on. I am writing to the women that had gotten pregnant unplanned, raped or any other circumstances even planned pregnancies. For the women that plan their pregnancies, the physical facts of this book will be helpful but the psychological aspect may or may not be relevant to you depending on each individual woman.

This book has help tips on parenting, health tips and issues dealt with during pregnancy and parenting for both baby and mommy. The psychological aspect of what is "O.K" to feel or not to feel during pregnancy and parenthood, the realization of loss of oneself as a person once pregnant and a parent, and the what to expect and deal with the first year of parenthood. Also help tips for dads to understand the mom as well as guidelines to have a functioning household once the baby arrives. Information on vaccines and other alternative medicine.

To the single dad that is left without a wife due to any circumstances here is a helpful guide to get you through your first year. Kudos to you and your bundle of love.

* *This book is not a medical book so please take your baby to a pediatrician for any treatment or illness and consult with your pediatrician before doing any tips that I have received and given to you.*

Are You Ready?

Ever wonder if you are ready to add on to your family? Well here are a few things from experienced moms to think about to help you decide if you are ready or not ready for an addition to your family. Do you look at a baby and say, "Oh, how cute! I want one!" Do you say, "Babies are so cute! I can't wait to have one!" If this is you speaking, well, I hate to break it to you, but *you're not ready*!

Let's get real here. The word *baby* only applies for a very short amount of time. How long? Four months. After that, the child is an infant until he or she is a year old, at which point he or she becomes a toddler. This seems like a long period, but it flies by before you can blink. Unreal? Yeah … no, it's not. You are so tired and sleep deprived through those four months; they come and go so fast that when you realize it, you don't have a baby anymore. In your mind, you are saying to yourself, *"What happened?"*

The reality is that you need to be ready and really want a child—a person in your life to raise, teach, and help become a respectable human being, an asset to the human race and society. You will have more time with a child than a baby. This is the thought that needs to go through your mind before you get pregnant. Are you ready and willing to do whatever it takes to raise a child? Do you see yourself with a child or only holding a baby? Take your time and think about it before making a move on this. Read this book! I hope it will open your eyes to the reality of what really happens with a baby/child and help you make an informed decision about whether you are ready to deal with it.

When I Found Out

I am going to share my pregnancy story and experiences in hopes that other women can relate and realize that it is okay to feel *different*. I was one of those women who felt *different*. When I found out I was pregnant, I was just finishing up graduate school, planning to become a professor at a university. I must admit that I cried and cried and, well, I cried some more when the little blue line showed up. I was not yet married to my fiancé, and we were in troubled times. I felt I did not have my life together just yet and was not ready to have a child come into this world. Though I did not think my life was over or blame the baby, I did feel cheated in life and just a year too short. I knew I was not going to be able to get a job anywhere because of the pregnancy and really had to make a decision on my relationship. My main focus became creating a family for my new baby and making sure I finished my master's so that when I could or wanted to go back to work, I had the education to do so with ease.

I was petrified by all these decisions I had to make so quickly. Internally, I still needed more time, but I did not have it physically. I am thankful to God that I am a fertile woman because I know some women have issues or may not be fertile at all. But I was still not at the place where I wanted to be before bringing a child into this world. My first decision was to get married. Some women choose differently, and that is okay too, no matter what people may tell you. My decision was my own. I did what I felt was right for me. Other women may think differently, and that is okay.

Through planning a wedding and finishing up my thesis, I realized that I did not enjoy pregnancy like women told me I should. Some women like being pregnant and actually enjoy it—well, not me. I'm one of the women who did not enjoy being pregnant. I thought I was a bad mother or horrible person for feeling that way, but I soon found out that I wasn't the only one who felt that way. Other women feel that way too, and if this is you, I want you to know that it is okay. No, it does not mean you are a bad person or mother. I mean, come on, you lose total control of your body, all these nauseating things start to happen to you, you are totally uncomfortable, and the list goes on. Why would you like it? Some women enjoy it or don't have such a bad experience with it. Lucky them!

I'm not going to sit here and say I had a bad pregnancy, because I didn't—well, not based on some of the horror stories I have heard from other moms. For example, some moms have morning sickness (which is not just in the morning; it's more like all day or at any part of the day) the entire duration of their pregnancy. Some have complications, and the list goes on. My pregnancy was pretty easy in itself; the only thing was that I had pubic symphysis diastasis. This is a condition in which the hormone relaxin causes the pelvis (pubic bone) to loosen. This is good for delivery, but in my case, the separation was exaggerated and moved incorrectly, which caused a great deal of pain in my sciatic nerve. This started at the fourth month of my pregnancy and got worse as the baby got bigger because of the weight and pressure on the nerve. This made me miserable. I was in a great deal of pain all the time. I was just not enjoying this miracle that was occurring in my body because of it.

Though I was in considerable pain, I still forced myself to exercise as much as I could without hurting myself. I walked and did arm exercises with bands in a mommy exercise group, which was my support group through this experience. I learned a lot from these mommies and made some new friends. Finding a support group for expecting moms and new moms was the best decision I made. I was able to talk to other moms and get feedback. They told me what worked for them and what didn't. I did ask a lot of questions because I was scared. I wondered how my life would change and if I would be a good mother.

I realized that I had started to become angry and gain resentment toward my husband. Now, I know that hormones change and can make pregnant women act a little "off," but I was more upset at myself, as well as angry at my husband for "doing this to me" when I wasn't ready. I didn't want a baby at this point in my life. I knew it was not the baby's fault, so I had to steer myself away from that and really focus on my emotional situation. I felt like a bad person for feeling this way. I felt a big burden on my shoulders and like I was trapped with a chain around my ankle.

I started therapy with my husband for this reason and other marital issues we were having. I was angry at him for "doing this to me" when I did not want it yet. I was also angry because his life didn't seem to change, but mine did, drastically, from what I ate to how I slept to what I could and could not do. I was angry for having to take care of someone again. I realized that this went back to my childhood. I grew up helping to care for my grandparents, whom I lived with until the age of nineteen, when my grandfather, the last of the elderly in my house, passed away. I did feel sad he was gone, but at the same time, I experienced a sense of freedom from responsibility for caring for someone else.

Now, starting to get my life together as an adult only eleven years later, I had ended up pregnant. I had to do it again! Ugh! Is that a horrible thing to say? I spoke to my therapist about it, and she let me know that it was okay to feel that way. I was also afraid of "losing myself," losing the person I had worked so hard to become. Maybe this is the way you feel. Maybe you feel the weight of responsibility only on your shoulders, or maybe you are alone and afraid. Whatever the case, it is okay to feel this way. Not everyone is "super happy" about being pregnant. We all have different emotions about it.

Here is how I was able to let go of that emotion.

Step 1: I recognized that it wasn't the baby's fault, so I was not going to blame the baby or hurt the baby in any way. I had to deal with this on my own without anyone knowing (my pregnancy secret) at the time. My baby was not going to be a burden to me; he or she was going to be a gift and miracle that I would get to enjoy and have fun with. Yes, he or she would be someone I had to care for but in a different way.

Once I had that under control in my mind, I was able to move on to Step 2: I had to mourn the death of me. What do I mean by that? In reality, yes, the me I knew as my own individual person—my carefree self—had died, and I had to be ready and willing to bury her. Did I cry? Oh boy, did I! For a few days really. The thought of me never being the same just devastated me. It was a terrible thought. *Why did this happen to me now? I wanted a family, just not right now.* I wasn't ready to bury myself yet. I wanted to still be me and worry about myself, *just me*! Yes, I know it was a selfish thought to have, but it's true and I'm not going to lie about it. I wasn't ready myself for this life-changing experience. If something like this happened to you, it's okay to feel this way.

Well, I guess God had other plans for me, which I was fighting to accept. When I was ready to lay my "old self" to rest and embrace the "new me," still being the person I was but having a permanent buddy to deal with and enjoy life with, I drew my experience on paper. You see; I am an artist. I was in art school getting my master's in painting, so I did what I knew best. I drew on a sheet of paper what it was to be with the ball and chain and what I thought it would be like to have a child and care for it like I did my grandparents. On another sheet, I drew the old me on one side of the paper and the new me enjoying the baby on the other. How would I maintain my identity with this child? I was not going to let my life come to an end. This wasn't a punishment; this was a new adventure, and I would get to have my child enjoy life with me.

On the third sheet of paper, I wrote down in one column the things I did as a single person. In the other column, I wrote down the things I could supplement my life with; certain things that I could no longer carelessly do I substituted with things that I could do with or without my child. These were things that still remained "me." For example, I used to pick up and go travel wherever I wanted, whenever I wanted. I could no longer do that, but I knew if I needed a getaway, I could plan a vacation with my family or if I wanted to be alone, I could go get my manicure and pedicure done and have some "me" time. Another option would be to go to the spa for a day, things of that nature. The list went on and was pretty extensive; I kept going until I felt good enough to stop.

Once I finished those drawings and my list, I was able and ready to "bury" myself. I got the drawing that had the ball and chain, took it outside, prayed, and let myself go. I burned the drawing in a fire pit and with it went my "old self "into the sky. It was a relief; the weight lifted off my shoulders, and I was ready to embrace my baby. Now, this does not mean I was happy to be pregnant or anything of the sort; I was just not going to be miserable about having this child anymore. The rest of the feelings were still there. I was still annoyed that it was a year too soon in my book. I still felt cheated a year. I still felt like I worked so hard for three years to get my master's and now what? Would it be in vain? Would I be able to get back to doing what I had set out to do? Would my goals change? Who knew? But there was one thing I knew: no one could take my education and talent from me. How I used it or even whether I chose to use it was my prerogative, but I had earned my master's. I achieved a goal no one in my family had achieved, and that made me proud of myself. My child would be able to look up to me for my achievement, and that made me feel better. Do you have something you're working on or you are proud of? You can pass that on to your child.

Now don't get me wrong; it's not like I didn't enjoy my pregnancy at all. I did have great moments, but that's what they were for me: *moments*. For example, the first time I felt the baby move, the times when I massaged my cocoa-butter cream on after the shower and the baby reacted to the feeling, when I would watch or hear anything that had nice singing or classical music and the baby would respond to it by dancing in my belly—all of these experiences no one else in the world was going to experience with my baby but *me!* How special is that? I got to know when my baby was happy, angry, bothered, sleeping, or just playing. No one knew that but me, and that made me feel special.

I do have to admit one thing. When I found out the sex of the baby, I was disappointed; well, I had hoped for and dreamed of a girl, and of course, my husband wanted a boy. Ever since I was a little girl, I had always wanted a girl. I even had dreams that I had a girl. One day, I was shopping for neutral baby stuff with my mom and we were at the checkout line when something told me it was a boy. I was, to be honest, a bit bummed out, but I wasn't going to let myself feel that way just yet because I did not know for certain. I did tell my mother that although I so wanted a girl, I had a feeling it was a boy. When it was the time to find out the sex of the baby, the ultrasound technician looked at me and said, "What did you want?" with a funny look on his face and a sarcastic tone in his voice.

I said, "I wanted a girl, but now I know it's a boy."

He looked at me and said, "Yes, you are right; it's a boy!"

My husband and mother were with me at that moment, and both of them were jumping for joy and screaming with excitement. All the while, I just lay there on the table looking at the ultrasound with my mouth open in shock and, well, disappointment. In my mind, I was devastated. *What am I going to do with a boy?* I thought to myself. I wanted a girl. Was I a bad person for thinking this? I was sad I did not get what I had always dreamed about. I then realized that, no, I was not a bad person or bad mom-to-be. I was just a person with a crushed dream. It is okay to feel that way. I knew I had to get over this and connect with my new son, so I went to the store and bought some boy baby clothes that I thought were cute and some newborn shoes. After I did that, I felt so much better and started to really connect with him. I had my own moment alone with my baby inside me, and we bonded. I no longer felt devastated or disappointed. I was open to the idea of a boy and decided I was going to raise him to be a man of God, to know and do all the things I ever wanted in a man for one lucky lady in his future. I was going to do this to the best of my ability and with God's help to mold my son. On a side note—I am so happy to have had a boy. He is the joy of my life, and I would not have it any other way. What an easy boy I have. I am so blessed he was born healthy, happy, and amazing. He is the inspiration in my life. Every day, I wake up eager to see his smiling face and hear his view on the world with a smile. No matter how I feel, when I look at him, he makes me happy and makes me love life.

Birth Story

Every birth story is different and extremely personal, but there are some things that remain the same. You plan or go into labor, and you end up with a baby; everything else in between goes very differently for each mother. Though the end result is the same, not all women feel the same once they meet their beautiful new baby. What do I mean? Well, you hear birth stories from other women or your mother, aunts, etcetera, and they tell you what they went through; they saw when the baby came, it was instant "love at first sight," and they say things like, "Oh what a wonderful feeling it was." The list can go on, but what happens when you don't feel that way? Why do you feel differently? Is that wrong? Is something wrong with you? Well, I'll get into that in my birth story in hopes that you will understand and know you are not alone.

I had a planned C-section. Yes, I planned it, and I am not ashamed of it! I am not one of those women who need a gold star next to me because I had it naturally. *Nope!* Not me! If you are a woman who did it naturally, hats off to you! I am glad you were able to accomplish that. There is nothing wrong with natural or C-section birth. Women who had C-sections for whatever reason are no less of a mother and no better or worse of a mother. One experience no less traumatizing to the body than the other. The end result you give birth and have a baby just the same. Now, as I mentioned earlier, I had a condition called pubic symphysis diastasis, which made life in general for me very painful. The thought of moving my body or getting dressed made my toes curl from the pain. Plus, my baby was a big one with a big head. If I would have delivered naturally, I could have permanently damaged myself and gone through more pain in labor than a regular woman. Of course, I did not want that and was not going to have to deal with that and a new baby, so C-section it was.

A lot of my friends asked me to give them specific details on the process of a C-section because they were thinking of it too. Since no book out there goes through it step-by-step, I'm going to tell you how it went for me so that if you are thinking about it, you will be prepared. At the end of the day, it is a surgery, but to be honest, most people make it out to be a bigger deal than it is. If not, then I can handle a lot. But, hey, why don't you be the judge of it and see if you can deal with it or not? Like I said, every woman is different.

A week before the scheduled date for my delivery, I went with my husband to finalize my plans, register myself, and give all the information to the hospital so I would not have to do it once I got there. They then took me to a room where they went over allergies and my medical history and gave me some instructions on what to do the night before delivery.

This entails no eating after 12:00 a.m. the night before, not even water. (This is so that when they give you the anesthesia, you do not get sick or vomit if you have a reaction to it.) You also need to *make sure two nights before, you shave whatever you want to shave!* Why?

Well, you can't shave the night before just in case you cut yourself and get an infection. When you shower the night before, you *must* shower with a specific gel they give you to sterilize your body and you cannot use perfume, deodorant, cream, or anything you normally put on your body. You must be completely clean and sterile! You must shower again in the morning before going to the hospital the same way you did the night before. You cannot wear makeup—no, nothing on you—before the surgery.

Now, if you plan on a natural delivery and things get complicated—like many women have had to go through—do not worry; none of these steps pertain to you.

They take you to another room after briefing you on all this, and they take some blood and urine samples and send you home.

The day of delivery, well, what can I say? I, of course, did not sleep the night before because of nerves. It was my last night as just me and us as a couple; from that moment on, we would be a family, our own unit that had been created by my husband and me. It really was a big deal and a very powerful moment. So I got ready and went to the hospital. As soon as I got there, they took me right in. I changed into my gown and took everything off, no jewelry or any clothes except the gown and socks they provided. They then put these wraps on my legs to keep circulation going. Soon thereafter, they took my blood pressure, took some more blood out, and put the IV in me. My husband was asked to step out, and I was there answering some personal questions. Once that was done, he was allowed back in, and the anesthesiologist came to visit when they were ready for me.

At this point, I was scared. I had never gone through any sort of injection like this before, especially one that I could not see. (Now, if you are having an epidural, it will be a similar process, but you will be going through contractions while this goes on.) The anesthesiologist listened to the concerns I had from hearing the horror stories and my fear of needles. After a few laughs, he assured me all would be okay and he would walk me step-by-step through what he was going to do.

After we had waited for about two hours for my doctor to arrive, they escorted my husband out and me into the delivery room. I walked into the room where everything was sterile around 12:30 p.m. I looked around to see where everything was and where they would put the baby, and then I saw my bed. Yeah, this thing was the size of my back; it was very small in width. My first thought was, *This is it?* Yep, it sure was. I sat on this bed facing one of the nurses; she took my blood pressure and left the strap on. It would continue to take it throughout the procedure. Then she said, "Okay, now slouch over as much as possible and put your head down." At this point, I thought she was going to hold me down, and she said, "No, that is only when you're in labor and we have to put the epidural in while you have contractions." So I held my breath and prayed, "God, please be with me and the doctors who work on us for all to be at your will and come out great!"

The anesthesiologist said to me, "Okay, we are ready!"

He cleaned my back and patted it dry. He then put tape on my back. (I'm guessing it had the spine on it so he knew where to put the anesthesia.) Then he said, "Okay, take a deep breath; you're going to feel a pinch." Usually, when a doctor tells me that, it hurts more than a pinch! But in this case, he was right; it hurt less than giving blood or getting a mosquito bite. (When you're having contractions in a natural birth with an epidural, I have heard from other moms you do not feel the pinch from the needle.) I did feel the anesthesia go in but then quickly went numb. I know he went again two more times. I did feel an electric shock in my right leg that did hurt a bit, but that was the worst of it really. Now for me to say this is big because I am a wimp when it comes to stuff like this. He then took off the tape and laid me down. I quickly went numb in my legs. Ha! That was a strange feeling, not being able to move them. Then, as it gradually went up my belly, the anesthesiologist kept checking me with a dull needle to see how different I felt with touch.

When I was ready and numb, they put the catheter in—I did not feel anything but some pressure—and taped it to my leg. Then they put up the curtain and put this gel on my belly. I was numb. I felt the gel being put on but I did not feel the actual temperature of the gel; it felt warm. But in reality, the doctor told me it was *freezing* cold. (I think they do this to minimize the blood flow so you do not bleed out, but this is my nonmedical guess.) They put another tape-like thing on my belly. Then they started the surgery. I was shaking through the entire procedure; I think it was because of the freezing gel and the anesthesia combined. I did not see anything, nor did I feel anything.

My husband came in when they had started. He kept talking to me throughout the procedure and so did the anesthesiologist, guiding us step-by-step. They cut the skin, break your water, that I did somewhat feel some liquid over me but very minimal and without pain. What I did feel was that the baby moved upward toward my ribs when they were ready to take him out. They pushed him down and pulled him out. I did feel an uncomfortable pressure then. *Wow!* What a relief! He was out! And I heard the best cry ever. Our son was born. Some friends have asked me to describe the pressure. If I were to explain it to someone who has not gone through it, what it would be like? This is what I can say to come close to it, and it will be a bit strange. It's like if you have been constipated for a few days and you finally let it out, that feeling of relief and having your body back to normal, that gasping for air and the sigh of having it done!

My husband then went to take pictures of the baby as they were cleaning him up to show him to me while they started to close me back up. I did smell something being burned; that was the doctor welding my skin together. It sounds painful but it was not. Recovery was less painful, no infections and healed beautifully. Some people ask me if the anesthesia affected the baby in any way. My answer is no. From the test they take when a baby is first born with highest most impossible score a 10/10 points my son got an above average of 10/9. Normal is 9/9, he was not affected in any way, nor was he drugged out. When the baby was cleaned and brought to me, he was alert and very curious about this new world. I was expecting to feel what I had been told I was supposed to feel, love at first sight. Well, I did not feel that; after all, I had just been introduced to this new person. I don't feel love at first sight when I meet a new person; that has to grow—for me anyway. I wondered if I was a bad person or mother for feeling that way. But in reality, I'm not; many mothers have felt the same way. My first thoughts were, *Wow, is he really mine? Did he just come out of me? This person was made inside me! Who does he look like? OMG, I am totally responsible for this person from now on! What a responsibility! We are parents!*

I knew the connection and the love would occur later on between us, though it was love at first sight for my husband—at least that's what he tells me. I kissed the baby, and they took him away to the nursery. My husband went with him. I was there still in the surgery room being sewn up, talking to the nurses. When they finally finished, they put me on a board and slid me onto the rolling bed to transfer me to recovery. It took me two and a half hours to be able to move my legs. That was the goal I had to meet in order to go to my room. Boy, was it strange to try to move my legs and discover I couldn't! The connection from brain to limb was not working at the moment. I was offered painkillers that were strong, but I knew I wanted to breastfeed, so I did not take them. I also knew the side effects and did not want to be drowsy when

I saw our baby again. I only took Motrin 800; it was my other option every six hours.

When I finally moved my legs, I was transferred over to my room where they brought in our baby and I held him and fed him for the first time. It was a special moment, but that is when your motherly instinct kicks in and it just becomes natural, like it was meant to be all along. I was then able to eat ice chips and see how my body reacted to them. Then I was allowed water and finally able to eat light food. Remember, I hadn't eaten since midnight the night before, and by the time I had some ice chips, it was 6:30 p.m. I was starving! I had real food at 9:00 p.m. that evening.

The reason people sometimes say you don't sleep at the hospital is not just because of the baby needing something; it's also because they come every three hours to check on you. If it's not food, it's taking your vitals or giving you whatever meds you need or even taking your blood every morning at 6:00 a.m. Now add that to a baby needing to feed and be changed every two hours or so, and there you have it—*no sleep*! Some people have the nurse take the baby, but for me, I found it pointless. I could sleep with my baby and not have to really move at night to feed, just pop out a breast and relax until he needed changing, instead of having a nurse wake me up every time he was screaming for food, which was very often. This was more calming for me and less stressful on all of us.

I have to tell the truth because no one tells you this. Mainly all you hear is the "Oh, how wonderful it is," and yes, it is true; it is wonderful! *But* there is another side to the story than what is normally told because no one wants to appear to be a bad mom. Well, let's talk about the elephant in the room, shall we? Let's see what really goes on with a woman who has become a new mom. I wish I would have known to be a little bit more prepared and aware of these things when they did happen, *and they will happen*!

The love did take a few days to kick in. I mean, everything was just so overwhelming, and I wondered, am I the only one? Well, my therapist said that it was normal and it would happen when I was ready. Some women take longer than others. She was right; it did happen, and it was so special too. I was home feeding him alone, and I took one look at his beautiful face and said, "Wow, I can't imagine my life without him. I love him so much, words cannot explain it." Of course, there were tears involved—and they come even to this day, just thinking back on that special moment. It was a connection between him and me that was like no other. Then a bond was built that will never be broken nor compared to what I have with anyone else. When you love someone else more than you can say and there is a love greater than the one you have for yourself, it is unbelievable. Pretty much what I am saying is you will learn the meaning of *love* when you have your baby. You think you may know what love is, but in reality, you only know a little glimpse of what it truly is.

You think you love your family, parents, spouse, and so on. Think *again*! Those are some aspects of love that you know, but the true meaning and what it feels comes at the arrival and connection with your own baby. I am a Christian woman. That was when I officially learned how God loves His son Jesus. I could only imagine what he felt when he had him die on the cross for all of our sins. Because he is perfect in every way, he was able to do that. It shows how much God and Jesus love us all. *Like his children.* Me … I am an imperfect human and would not *ever* be able to do that for a bunch of sinning people I do not know; I could not have my baby, whom I would give my life for, die for them. That in itself is utterly amazing! Only God can do that. You will understand that when you hold your baby.

Now What?

Congratulations! You're pregnant! Well, to most women, that is a great thing; to others, it's a surprise but still a blessing. Either way, it shows that you are fertile. For some women, that is not the case, so count it as a blessing. Now that you have gotten over the plus sign or the blue line, the next big question is, *now what?* Yep, your life has officially changed forever, assuming you are going to proceed with the pregnancy. This is a life changer. Your life will be different from this moment on and for the rest of your life. *Whew!* That's not a lot of responsibility ... Noooooo! Well, now that you have realized that, what do you do? The first step is to tell your significant other. If there is one or someone you trust. After that, start eating healthy food because whatever you eat, the *nutrients are going to your baby.* You are *not eating for two*; your baby just gets the nutrients. You may need to eat smaller amounts more frequently or a little more of a portion in your main meals and have healthy snacks in between. Drink an abundance of water! It doesn't matter if you pee every five minutes, you need it and so does your baby!

Now that all that is out in the open, you still may have mixed feelings. Let's talk about the elephant in the room, shall we? This is the load of responsibility that just landed on your shoulders. This baby/fetus depends on you to survive and make it to the birth. No pressure! You need to make sure you are always safe, have minimal stress, are healthy, eat well, exercise to maintain your weight, and give off good hormones and endorphins to your unborn baby. Talk about a change of life, huh? You also have to maintain your ordinary life as well until the baby comes. That's not a lot … Ha!

This can be overwhelming for most women—at least it was for me. The thought that I would never be an "I" again but would be a "we" from then on was frightening. This was not including my partner because that of course makes you a "we," but it is not like this "we." This was a "we" that with or without a partner/spouse would always be. The death of who I used to be was hard to swallow because I had finally gotten to understand and know her. I had to figure out who I was *now* and who I would *become* once the baby arrived. Well, the second part, you won't know until the day your baby arrives, but in the process of pregnancy, you also change in the way you see life and how you behave, as well as what you think about or talk about. It is usually all about baby, baby mode in gear!

For some women, this shift is harder than it is for others, but whatever the feeling, it is okay and normal. It doesn't make you a bad person if this shift is hard for you; you are not alone! My suggestion is to go and see someone to talk to, maybe a friend or a therapist; it might help you better cope with this change in your life. After all, you just got hit with a ton of responsibility, fear of what is to come, and a love you cannot understand yet is normal. Let's add the fact that the *you* that you know is *no longer* and, well, *you will never be the same.* Smile; after all, it is a good thing. Whether you can see it yet or not, it will pay off.

Now that we got that out of the way, what are the things you're going to need as essentials at first? Well, since the economy isn't all that great, and for most people, money is tight, you are going to have to fight off the urge to buy your baby everything you see. I know it's hard because it's your baby and your baby deserves the best and everything you can give him or her! But your pocket may disagree with the love you have for your little bun in the oven. So let's be *practical* and do a little of both. Let's come to a *compromise* on the things your baby will need immediately and the luxuries you want for your little one. Every family is different, so if you have the means to spoil your baby, *go ahead.* If not, don't feel bad. Your little one doesn't know the difference and does not need much for the first few months.

Let's make your practical registry, and you can move on from there as your little bundle of joy grows up. Your main items and essentials are pretty basic. I am going to tell you what I picked out, and in no need do you have to choose the same; it is just my choice. Everyone is different and does things her own way, but if you need guidance, here is a list.

Bigger items:

1. **Bassinette** (I chose a co-sleeper it made it easier to get the baby in and out for late night breastfeeding's and easier for moms who had a C-section. If you are not breastfeeding this one is optional you may just get the crib if you do not want your baby to sleep next to you.)

2. **Changing table and laundry basket** (I chose one that had both in one it made changing easy) People also choose just to have the changing mattress on a dresser. Either is fine. Don't forget the *covers for the mattress!*

3. **Rocker Chair** (Invest in this! It is expensive but it is the item most needed and where most of your time will be spent on *it needs to be comfortable*! I prefer a *recliner and rocker* so *you* can be comfortable too!) Make sure you get the *ottoman* that comes with it. Your comfort depends on it!

4. **The Swing** (*Your new best friend!*) get one that is comfortable, has soothing sounds and has some type of stimulation like a mobile or a mirror for the baby to be amused. This item will help with the baby's vestibular system. Give you some free time and a nice place for a nap.

5. **Baby Activity Gym** (This will give you a break from holding the baby and place of learning and experimenting for your little one; with music and stimulation this gym is great for newborns and infants)

6. **Baby Seat Bouncer/ Vibrator** (Google this to get the one you like.) Why is this necessary? Well do you want to shower? If you strap the baby in this seat you can bring your baby into the bathroom with you and you have peace of mind to shower with baby in your supervision. These usually vibrate and/or play music for the baby.

7. **Breast Pump** You may purchase one or rent one from the hospital if you are not sure if you can or want to pump. This is used so that mommy is not the only one feeding the baby. Family and friends may also enjoy feeding the baby giving mommy a break.

8. **Bottle Warmer** *Necessity!* This makes your life easier when warming a bottle late night or early morning. I mean would you like to only have cold milk if you are bottle feeding? If you pump your breast milk and freeze it for later use; you need to use a warmer to warm it up within 3minutes. Or you can use a pot and pan and wait to boil water and then put the bottle in it, this will take you a lot longer.

9. **Wipe Warmer** Now this some parent's use and others do not. But think about it, your baby is being wiped down at 2 or 3 a.m. after a feeding and he/she is wet but still warm. Now you are going to wipe down your little one with something that is really cold! What do you expect the outcome of that will be? *Crying!* The warmer will be a smoother more pleasant transition for your bundle of joy. Now, I'm not saying to take it with you or anything like that; they also need to get used to the wipe at any time and place, but at night and in the morning, it is a lot better to have a warmer; especially with boys. The warmer prevents accidents on your face if you know what I mean. The warmer makes the wipes feel better on your baby's face if you wipe them down. Try it yourself and see what it's like.

10. **Bottle Sterilizer** use after washing bottles by hand (unless you wash bottles in your dishwasher) you need to sterilize your baby's bottles, pacifiers, teethers' etcetera. It saves on your water bill later for the amount of times you have to do this nightly instead of running the dishwasher.

11. **Car Seat** how else are you going to take the baby home, or anywhere for that matter. Make sure your baby seat has all the safety features you want and need for your baby.

12. **Car Seat Protector** you don't want to ruin your car seats just because you have a baby seat in the back.

13. **Car Window Shade** poor baby; if they are in the back of the car with the sun hitting their face. How uncomfortable is that.

14. **Stroller** That too! You're going to need to get out of the house. *Duh*! Make sure you go to the store and try them all out. Each mom has her specifics on what she wants, needs or can handle. See if your baby store has a lifelike doll that weighs the weight of a baby and put it on the stroller to figure out if you can handle the stroller or not. It's very different with a baby in it than not.

15. **Baby Food Processor** unless you already have one that you use or you are not going to be making your own baby food then you do not need this item. If you are planning on making your own this is essential. You will need it by the time your baby is about four months. This is when you start adding puree to your baby's diet, then venture off into solids.

16. **Baby Carrier** this item will help you free up your hands while still caring for your little one. Especially if you have more than one child. That way you can tend to both children and do activities at the same time.

Smaller Necessities:

1. **Bottles** (*For breastfeeding and formula moms you do not want to be the only one having to feed your baby, you need a break too.*) (It is more practical to get the bigger 8oz. bottles because babies are hungry! Less bottles and more milk in the bigger bottles than the small ones. If you get the small ones it's better for water after the fourth month.) My preference:

I used all the brands to try them out and there are myths of latching on right if a baby uses a certain brand or type of nipple. Remember they are trying to get you to buy their product so depending on which one your baby likes best. It doesn't matter how the nipple on the bottle is your baby will always want the breast better than the bottle. If you start them off on level 1 until you stop breastfeeding it has the same consistency as your breast flow, if you go to a higher level, then your baby will find it easier to drink from the bottle than your breast; so your baby will want only the bottle. Some babies prefer some shaped nipples over others so you have to start with one kind to see if it works for your child. I chose a certain brand because of the nipple experience it does not get sucked in to the bottle while the baby is drinking, when using formula it usually gets clumped up with the water before warming and sometimes even a little after warming, the clumps may stay in the bottle and make its way into the nipple, where it may clog your nipple making it hard for your baby to eat; also your baby may even eat the clumps of formula because of this and that is not good. Most bottles may also produce air bubbles within the bottle giving your baby more gas and cause him/her to be colicky. *Dr. Browns* has the technology within the bottle straw to eliminate air bubbles and with the stopper it has within the bottle it prevents the formula clumps from getting in the nipple. Some mom's like other brands better but this was my choice. It's up to you on what you like best. Another bottle that has somewhat of the same system is the *Podee Baby Feeding System* it is a bottle with a straw connection that can be used in any position the baby is in. (*I do not get anything from naming brands just a* mom's knowledge to another what has worked best for my baby.)

2. **Bottle Brushes** these will help you clean those bottles that a sponge cannot get too.

3. **Baby Dish Soap** they are different than regular soap so please get this for your baby's bottles. They have less perfume and extra stuff that are not good for babies.

4. **Drying Rack** after you clean and sterilize the bottles you need to have a place to put them so they dry and are ready for use.

5. **Milk Storage Bags** If you are breastfeeding and you pump your milk you need these to store your milk in the freezer.

6. **Formula** If you are not breastfeeding, or if you are breastfeeding and use formula for the last feeding at night to have a longer night sleep. Babies will respond better to some formulas than others. It's a trial and error until you find the one that works best for your baby. Be sure to check the sugar amount in formula and in puree foods. Too much sugar can lead to other problems like irritability and lack of sleep.

7. **Bathing Tub/Hammock** Whatever you choose that works best for your sink and baby. (*I used a few different types, the best for me was the baby bath hammock while he was a newborn, and it was easy to use, store and keep clean. Once my baby grew out of it I used a baby bathtub.*)

8. **Bathing sponge/small washcloth** helpful for bathing baby's soft delicate skin with a bath soap of your choice. The washcloth is also good for boys when changing a diaper or in the bathtub, place it on his penis to prevent accidental spraying on you.

9. **Bath Towels** for newborns it is best to use a soft thin hooded towel because of their delicate skin and small bodies. All the other bath towels that are thicker with characters are best when the baby is older and bigger.

10. **Baby Shampoo and Body Wash** get something gentle for baby's skin. If your baby has eczema talk to your pediatrician to see what special soap to use.

11. **Baby Lotion** it is imperative you put lotion on your baby after a bath. You don't want your baby to have dry skin. If your baby has eczema there are special lotions for that too.

12. **Diapers and Wipes** Babies use about ten diapers a day sometimes more if they are newborn, so do the math ten diapers a day about one hundred and seventy diapers a week. Just think about the wipes! But don't think your little one will use a lot of newborn diapers they usually have a growth spurt and go from newborn to size one with in the first few weeks. Try using different brands of wipes on yourself before the baby arrives; that way you can figure out what you like on yourself instead on babies sensitive skin. Though you may need to try a few when the baby arrives if his/her skin does not agree with your first choice.

How many do you need?

Diapers & Clothes: To start off, your baby will use a lot of diapers so I would say to get *five* size one diapers of a box of at least one hundred and thirty diapers and up, and *five* size two diapers of the same. This will get you through your first month or two of your baby's life. If your baby is a preemie or under seven pounds at birth then you can get the newborn size diapers and clothes. Why do I say this? Well the baby grows so fast unless there is an issue or just a small baby that grows slower than normal; that if your little one is seven pounds and over newborn clothes and diapers go only to eight pounds max. So don't waste your money on something you may just have to return or never use or may just use once because it is too tight on your baby. A good tip: Wait till your sixth or seventh month ultrasound and find out the weight of your baby. If your baby is about six pounds by then do not waste your time and money on anything newborn; they just won't fit well. Your best bet would be to get anything from size one in diapers and zero to three months in clothes. That is what they use at the hospital anyways and it is more comfortable on your baby.

13. **Adult diaper pads** (This is a personal item, I have a boy so the accidents were more often than not; so; to avoid having to do laundry so many times a day or week I got these pads to line the changing table. When there was an *accident* it would wet the pad and it was easy to change, instead of having to change the cover of the changing table and do so much laundry.)

14. **Diaper Pail** Avoid not having the baby's room smell like a dirty diaper. Get a pail to keep the dirty diapers in one contained place.

15. **Diaper Pail Refills** you're going to need them. The most they hold is two hundred and forty diapers so you may last about a week and a half to two weeks with one. They usually come in a pack of four; which will be more economical.

16. **Diaper Changing Organizer** this is most helpful when changing the baby and having all your necessities next to you. If you have an area for you to change the baby that is

convenient then you may not need this item. Babies do wiggle a lot and it is very dangerous to leave them unattended while reaching for items. Some babies have fallen off the changing table because of this.

17. **Baby clothes** get comfortable clothes for your baby, they will be changed often due to spit up, vomit and diaper accidents. Shoes are not necessary but cute for pictures. Remember most of your day will be spent at home feeding, changing and sleeping for the first month or two.

18. **Bibs and burp cloths** essential unless you want to always be full of yucky stuff that *will* come out of your baby. At first your baby will only need the burp cloths for burping after a bottle or breast milk. But at two months old your baby will start teething. They do not necessarily have to have teeth but the teeth do start to move and that causes the baby to salivate more to the point that you will need to have a bib on at all times. *Get plenty of them you will need it. Unless you want to do laundry every two days.*

19. **Blankets** You do not want your little one to be cold or uncomfortable. (*For warmer climates the muslin material works best rather than the thicker ones.*)

20. **Swaddles** these are great to have to make nighttime easier. You will need two Small and two Medium. For the reason of if one is dirty and in the laundry you have the other as a backup. After the medium size your baby should be able to sleep on his/her own, if not there are always large sizes.

21. **Butt Ointment** good to have and put on the baby to prevent or eliminate diaper rash. Figure out which one works for your baby. Remember your baby's skin is super soft and sensitive at first so this is important to use when introducing diapers.

Some moms use coconut oil as a butt ointment for a more natural product.

22. **Teethers'** babies tend to start teething at two months of age. This does not mean that they have teeth but, that his/her teeth start to slowly move in and that really hurts and bothers them; so they will be a little bit on the cranky side. If you get a couple teethers' and put them in the fridge they will help with the uncomfortable feeling of this stage. (My favorites are the toothbrush banana, the toothbrush that slides on your finger from the medical kit (these rubber toothbrushes break the gums and its easier for the teeth to come in, these items make teething a little bit more tolerable and keeps teeth that come in clean. Susie the giraffe with handles works well too.)

23. **Medical Kit** this does not need any reason why, *you just need it!*

24. **Thermometer** some medical kits bring the normal one but now with technology a thermometer that can read your baby's forehead or the ear temperature is better and less bothersome to your baby if he/she is sleeping.

25. **Humidifier** you're going to need this. Babies get congested easily and you don't want your little one to linger with mucus in his/her chest for no reason.

26. **Hangers** some stores give you hangers with the baby clothes but some do not so a few hangers for your baby's closet is helpful.

27. **Diaper Bag** this goes without saying. This will be your new purse! Everything will be in this bag so make sure you like the color, make sure it's comfortable and you have plenty of compartments for all your baby's and your necessities.

28. **Baby detergent** there are plenty of baby detergents to choose from. Make sure you have this item, because regular items contain other chemicals that are harsher on baby's skin for the detergents.

• Your baby does not need any toys for they do not know how to move much or play for the first few months so that can be put aside after the third or fourth month. They will enjoy a soft stuffed animal or so and some teethers' and easy to chew on toys.

Once you have these essential items you are set for your baby's arrival anything else can be purchased once the baby is born and a few months old.

What You Really Need for the Hospital

This was a question I asked a lot. I got different answers depending on the mother; and well; the amount of children you are having at once. Roughly, this is what I took and what I really ended up using.

- Make sure you do your hands and feet before going to the hospital. It will be a while before you get to do them again, plus everyone will be looking at you.
- Anything you may need for the bathroom. (Toothbrush, toothpaste, face wash and creams, blow dryer, hair cap, shampoo, conditioner, body wash and sponge, razor, hair brush, clip or ponytail, coco butter lotion (your body needs it now more than ever), glasses/contacts, contact case and solution and some pajamas)
- Breastfeeding sleep bras (if you plan on breastfeeding) take one for each day you are at the hospital. I say this just in case you may want to change them and or have leaking accidents.

- Breastfeeding pads. Use them because you will leak and if you put ointment on your nipples it will stain your sleep bra.
- Nipple ointment your nipples will crack and hurt so take your ointment to make soothe them.
- Slippers and socks to sleep in. Remember your feet will swell no matter what delivery you have so make sure your socks will be big and not tight.
- You do not need normal underwear if you had a C-section. You will have a special under wear that is *fantastic*. As well as pads no matter how you deliver. Just use the ones at the hospital they are comfortable and save the ones you have for use at home.
- A going home outfit for you and your baby. (Have your partner follow this list too, but he can ware regular clothing not just pajamas daily.)
- Nursing bra to go home in.
- Make up to go home (you want to look presentable right?) Especially when the hospital takes your picture with the baby just before leaving.
- I-pad and charger (optional)
- Phone/ Charger
- Camera/Recorder
- Snacks you and your partner will be hungry!
- Soft jacket to go over pajamas some hospitals may be cold
- Remember your hospital will give you everything you need for the baby so take advantage of it and take as much as you can. Diapers, wipes, formula, ointment and pacifiers. Remember you are paying for all of this so take advantage.
- Take your own butt ointment if you feel more comfortable.

- If you have a girl bring your special cute hair bandana you want to put on her to go home or for pictures but let her be bandana free when not taking pictures. She is just born and her skin is very delicate these items may irritate her little head and be very uncomfortable.

- Remember every time the nurse takes your baby to check him/her, bathe, or do whatever they need to; they will change the outfit you have on your baby and put the hospital shirt on him/her when they return the baby back to you. Tip: Just leave the outfits for when you go home. The baby will be wrapped up in the blanket the entire time unless being changed so you will not need the cute clothes just yet. Especially, running the risk of losing an article of clothing like I did when they changed my son. Take advantage of the shirts and keep them; they will come in handy later on for fevers when they need to dress lightly. Save the hand mittens also for home the shirts have the mittens already.

- Socks for your baby if you like

- Spit up blankets

- Baby hats (in my case my son's head was too big for the hat's they have for newborns so thankfully I had my own)

- Baby Blankets (even though they gave us the hospital ones, I felt that it was more comfortable to sleep with the ones we got him at night, but that's just me.)

- Boppy Pillow (it will help you breastfeed and hold your baby)

- Your Pillow (it will be a lot more comfortable than the ones at the hospital)

- Small bag for your belongings if you go for a C-section it is easier to keep your stuff in it. Ex. Phone, glasses, camera, clothes that you take off before you go into surgery.

What Do Babies Cost Monthly?

Okay let's talk numbers here. How expensive are babies and what do they really need a month? Let's balance this out so that you can prepare and save; or just have an idea of how much you will be spending for your little one. These are items and prices taken from Amazon.com at the 2014 prices in the USA. These are just general items nothing in particular, just to have an idea. This list is for the first four months until you add baby food to the diet.

Diapers

Pampers Swaddlers Diapers Size 1 Economy Pack Plus two hundred and sixteen Count = $45.97 x three

(Based on one hundred and seventy diapers a week and ten diapers a day)

Wipes

BabyGanics Face, Hand & Baby Wipes, Fragrance Free, Contains Four- One hundred-Count Packs = $15.29

Butt Ointment

Burt's Bees Baby Bee Original Lotion, six Ounces (Pack of three) = $21.09

Formula *one can lasts roughly three days*

Baby's Only Organic Dairy Formula, 12.7 Ounce (Pack of six) = $68.92 x two = eighteen days

Similac Advance Infant Formula, Powder, 23.2-Ounces (Pack of six) = $149.88 x two

Earth's Best Organic Infant Formula with Iron, 23.2 Ounce Canisters (Pack of four) = twelve days = $89.99 x three

Similac Expert Care Alimentum Hypoallergenic Infant Formula, Powder, With Iron, 1-Pound (454 g) (Pack of Six) = $129.00 x two

* For every four ounces of water you need two spoonful's of formula (the ones that come with the formula). So if your baby takes an eight ounce bottle then you need four spoonful's of formula.

Roughly about three hundred and fifty dollars to four hundred and fifty dollars just on these items alone. That is if you do not have to do a fifty/fifty, which means half of the formula, you have and half of the Alimentum for babies with sensitive stomachs. This does not include any clothing or toys you may get; or if you do not give your baby formula then the amount may change.

Feeding

Babies go through transitional phases starting at four months of age. The first transition is from breast milk or formula to what we call "baby food," which is pureed food. Now you can make your own or buy some at the grocery store. Either way, it's a transition that your baby's body goes through, learning to eat more solid food that will keep him or her full longer. This is fun to taste in the mouth and feel with the hands, and they can discover a whole new world. Look for the baby-led weaning papers from your doctor's office to guide you on what to give your baby first and how long to make sure he or she does not have allergies to any foods. It is also good to see what a baby can have and what he or she cannot have, depending on the age of the baby.

Baby food runs about $1.70 for a pouch of organic baby food in 2014 in the United States. You go through about two to six a day, depending how many times you feed your baby food versus the bottle. You can save on baby food by doing it yourself if you have the time.

When the baby is six months of age, you can go from stage one, really fine puree, to stage two, less fine with more texture. This is the second transition. It is always fun to see how your baby reacts to different textures and foods. It allows you to see what your baby likes and dislikes. You may also be able to give your baby some solids that dissolve in his or her mouth or that are soft, like bread. Make sure your pediatrician agrees. If not, wait until your baby is a little older, like eight or nine months and move to stage three baby food which is more chunky puree.

At this point, you can teach your baby to pick up some baby puffs with a forefinger and thumb. You do this by putting dissolving baby puffs in a row in front of him/her in the high chair. Show the baby how to pick them up and watch him/her figure it out. Soon enough, your baby will be a pro at picking up items. This also teaches him/her independence in feeding him/herself, which makes your job easier.

Once your baby gets to be about six months, the amount of diapers diminishes to about six to eight diapers a day. The cost of formula and baby food also may be smaller because your baby will be more into solids. Babies eat more solids as they get older. By the time your baby is eleven months, he or she should be having only sixteen to twenty-four ounces of baby formula or breast milk and eating soft solids, something easy for your baby to eat if he or she only has a few teeth. Please make sure you and your pediatrician both agree this is where your baby should be.

The next transition is from textured puree to actual solid foods. By the time your baby is ten or eleven months old, he or she should be eating solid foods to chew on even if he or she only has a few teeth. It feels good on the gums and your baby needs the solid food to fill up. Your baby is more active at this point and needs more to sustain his/her growing and active little body.

By this time, your baby has become more independent in feeding him/herself, so feeding may be a little tricky. Here is a trick I figured out to make sure my baby got the nutrition he needed while still keeping feeding time fun and "independent" for him. My son would have tantrums during feeding time because he wanted to do it himself. But of course at this age, he still wasn't able to pick up the spoon and feed himself. So I would get some puffs or solid food and put it on his tray table, and I let him feed himself once (he may or may not have actually gotten it into his mouth); then I gave him a spoonful of whatever food I was giving him. That way, he was able to be "independent" and feed himself, and I was able to give him the nutrition he needed.

If your baby is on formula, speak to your pediatrician about doing a fifty-fifty formula with water and half almond/coconut/goat or hemp milk. This is a good way to transition your baby to only milk when he/she reaches the one-year mark. Then, he/she no longer needs the essentials in the formula. If you are going to continue to breastfeed, then do so by all means, but do regulate your baby so he/she gets a complete diet and is able to eat solids as a meal and not breast milk. Breast milk should be a side bar for nutrition at this point, not the main focus. But please consult with your pediatrician and make sure you both are on the same page. This is just a point of reference.

What No One Tells You

In this chapter, I have collected tips, suggestions, and home remedies for pregnancy and child care that no one talks about. It is where you find out about issues and things that may or may not happen to you and that pregnancy books just don't mention. This is also where I share tricks or ideas that have worked for other moms and are just passed down from mommy to mommy to make parenting easier.

I share old home remedies and new knowledge or alternative medicine on health care for both adults and babies. This in no way should be considered as medical guidance. Please consult with your pediatrician and doctor if any of these tips are new to you before doing them for yourself or your baby. What I share I have consulted with doctors about and have done myself, but everyone is different so please make sure your pediatrician is aware of what you are doing and is in agreement with it.

1. Your partner's desire for you may decrease during your last trimester because of fear of hurting the baby or simply because he does not see you the "same" way. In his eyes, you are a *mom* now, getting ready for birth, rather than his sexually attractive partner. This is totally normal but, unfortunately for the mom-to-be, not so fun.

2. During your last trimester, your hormones will skyrocket, and some women desire sexual contact more frequently.

3. Because of the elasticity in your muscles during pregnancy, you will find you are able to do things you were not able to do before as far as flexibility—this is true for most women anyway, if they are not suffering other conditions like pubic symphysis diastasis. So use this time and ability to your advantage!

4. Toward the end of your last trimester, your body begins to prepare for birth and so does your vagina. You or your partner may notice that your vaginal area begins to swell, preparing for delivery. This makes it hard to walk and cross your legs and leads to waddling in your walk, and sitting with your legs open becomes more comfortable.

5. Due to the changes in your physical body, hormones, and vagina, your vagina also may change in odor and taste, thus making oral pleasure unattractive to your partner. But do not worry; all of this does go back to normal after birth and your recovery.

6. When you or your baby is stung by a bee, according to some moms, putting garlic spread on the site makes it feel better.

7. When your child reaches four months of age, he/she begins to know how manipulation works and of course; wants your attention. Somehow, all, or the majority anyway,

of four-month-old babies have a "cough." No need to be alarmed if you notice this, unless it is a real cough; you will be able to distinguish the two. But all that your baby wants is your attention, and he/she is trying to get it the way he/she knows how.

8. For most babies who have diaper rash, parents try everything in the book to cure it. I found a cure after trial and error with creams and gel pads and so on. Please don't get me wrong; all babies are different, and mothers find different things that work, but what worked for my son when he had his diaper rash, which was very bad (it was red and raw with spots of blood), was *Burt's Bees Baby Bee Diaper Ointment (100% Natural)*. I put the cream on first, and then I put on *Burt's Bees Baby Bee Multipurpose Ointment (Petroleum Free)* on top of the cream. It not only made it better within twenty-four to seventy-two hours but also did not leave a white residue on his butt because of the multipurpose ointment.

9. When changing a boy and you get "baptized," what I found that works better than ruining your clothes and his is if you put a small washcloth on his "sprayer" while changing him. If he does have an "accident," the washcloth will soak it up and keep both of you clean.

10. Make sure you start a routine as soon as possible but not too soon either. The suggested time to start with some success is at three months of age. Babies are then able to sleep longer and take naps throughout the day. It will make life a lot easier. When they are younger than three months, it is harder because of feeding and off-sleep patterns coming from pregnancy, so stick to it and do not give up. There is a light at the end of the tunnel.

11. *The 5 S's:*

The 5 S's are from the book *The Happiest Baby on the Block*. I found that these steps in this book do help your baby sleep better.

1. Swaddling- Tight Wrapping
2. Side- Laying the baby on his/her side under your arms and the head in your hands.
3. Shushing- Shush loudly in the baby's ear or have white noise that is loud (vacuum, white noise app on your phone, etcetera.)
4. Swinging- Rhythmic, jiggling motion, for example, while gently rocking your baby from side to side in a small and quick movement. (*Do not shake the baby!*)
5. Sucking- Sucking on anything from your nipple or finger to a pacifier, usually the pacifier or your finger works if your baby is on his/her side with his/her head on your hands. If you were holding your baby facing your body, then your nipple would work. These steps must be done *exactly right* in order for it to work. You may find a detailed description of these steps in the book *The Happiest Baby on the Block or for a better visual watch the video.*

12. When you give birth and you start to carry your baby, your back may start to hurt. This is something no one tells you. Get yourself a chiropractor and massages frequently to help. It is due to the baby's growth weight, something your body is not used to supporting.

13. When you give birth, your stomach will get just a little smaller, but you will still have the baby belly. No worries, it will come off as the first month goes by.

14. Your stomach muscles change during pregnancy. It will take a while for your stomach to go back to normal. You will notice that your abdominal muscles have a gap in the middle. That is due to them spreading to make room for the baby. If you do exercises for your stomach and Kegels for your vagina, you will get them both back into place and normal.

15. Realize that a few things that were normal to you before the baby are now a luxury. Like what? Well, like *sleep* for sure! Try not sleeping for four days with a baby screaming for food or a changing every two hours and try to function in your daily life with chores, work, or anything you normally do. See how easy that is. Taking a shower daily (If you do this, you are doing great! Even every other day is great too!) maybe washing your hair or even shaving your legs, believe it or not, will become luxuries. Eating anything before 2:00 p.m. is too. Why? Well, you are so busy with the baby with feeding, changing diapers and clothing, and putting him/her down to sleep that by the time you check your watch, it is 2:00 p.m. and you have yet to eat a thing. Once your baby is about three to four months of age and starts to grab, watch out for your earrings. He or she may just pull them off or hurt your ear. Jewelry is also a luxury because babies like to bite it, pull on it, and break things. Staying clean? Yeah, that doesn't exist anymore. When you go out, take a change of clothes for yourself too. Talking on the phone? Ha-ha! Yeah, there you have it; you won't remember the last time you had a conversation without a crying baby or a babbling baby. If

you have help, congratulations, your life will be a *little bit* easier. Wearing *anything* strapless is a forgotten luxury only used on date nights if you have them because you're always carrying the baby. Watch out if you wear something like that; you may just give an unwanted peep show. Watching your favorite shows on TV, well, you just jumped to the baby channel, cartoons, and musical TV. Make sure you have TVO or a recorder so you can watch your shows once the baby is sleeping. This helps in the middle of the night when you're feeding and need to stay up too. Let's not forget reading a book. Now, that is a luxury.

16. When going on an outing with a newborn, make sure you have plenty of diapers, at least six in the bag to be safe and three to four changes of clothes because they will get dirty from spit-up or a wet or dirty diaper. As the baby gets older, you will not need as much and you can adjust from there. Usually, it's a good idea to take at least one or two changes at all times.

17. *This is so important and so true I have to reemphasize it.* No one tells you that you know what love is when your baby is born. You think you love your mate or family; think again! You will know what love is when your baby is in your arms, and you will reevaluate your love for everyone else. The love for your baby is so unbelievably great that words do not do it justice. It is overwhelming, it is unstoppable, and momma lion will come out if any danger or thought of danger comes to your baby. This will really be an eye-opener for you the first time it occurs.

18. Know that a woman changes three times in her life. Who she is before the baby, who she becomes when she finds out she is

pregnant and throughout the pregnancy, and once more when the baby arrives. This is a lot for most women because it's so much in a year's time that it can be overwhelming. That too is okay, and you will get used to the new person you have become when the baby arrives in due time. You will realize what you now will and will not tolerate, who you let close to your baby and yourself, what you like and do not like, and what your morals, principles, and values really are, because you have to pass them down to your baby and raise him or her the way you want your baby to be raised.

19. Once you have your baby, you will realize that some things in your closet will not fit or be the same ever! I'm not talking about your maternity clothes, which you are still in. I'm talking about when you lose the baby fat and you shrink back down. This may happen to you. Some women gain a half an inch in shoe size and lose all their previous shoes. Other women, like me, have the bone structure in their chest cavity widen, going from, for example a thirty-two to a thirty-four in bra size, meaning all my bras and shirts went from a small to a medium. This can also happen in your hips and change your jeans and pants sizes from (for me) a twenty-six to a twenty-seven-inch waist Therefore, all my pants, skirts, dresses, jeans, and even underwear did not fit anymore. I went from a small to a medium here too. I think this realization and acceptance was and still is the hardest to swallow. Some things you can't help and will never be the same. (Swallow hard and think positively! New wardrobe!) If you happen to go back to everything before pregnancy like normal consider yourself the few and a very lucky woman.

Ever wonder why you see a mom with a baby wear the same clothes twice or a few times in a row? Guilty! The reason behind that is when you get out of maternity clothes and into "regular" clothes, you still are very limited in what you can wear. Why? Well, the shirts have to meet certain criteria. Can I breastfeed? Is it easy to do so? Will my baby get tangled up in it? Will it rip due to carrying my baby? Will I have to fuss with my outfit to keep it from falling off? Tube tops are definitely out of the question. For pants, skirts, and dresses, can I squat down and get up easily to retrieve dropped pacifiers or toys? Will I be able to hold, pick up, or put down my baby and diaper bag? Is this comfortable not only for me but for my baby to feel as well? Is it too see-through so I will be showing more than I want to? Will this get too dirty from spit-up or anything else that comes out of my baby?

All of these questions are the ones you come across every day picking your clothes when you have a little one. That is why exercise clothing is very popular among mothers, and, hey, if you find something that meets all these requirements, then stick to it. The reason behind why moms wear the same thing over again a few times is it's just easier and less to think about.

20. Some children between the ages of six months and two years old go through something called Roseola. This is a viral infection that your baby can contract if someone coughs on him/her or if your baby plays with a toy that an infected baby had. Either way, it is very common and nothing to fear. For everything that is medical, please consult with your pediatrician to make sure your baby is okay. This is so you

do not freak out when you realize something is going on. See, roseola starts off with a very high fever, but if you're this far along, your baby has been teething by now so your first thought is that he or she is teething. You give him or her baby Tylenol and put a cold, wet cloth on the baby's forehead and neck. The fever will eventually break, but if it persists on day two and three, you may begin to worry. Well, it may be Roseola. It starts with a fever for three days, and then it stops. The baby will then develop a red rash all over his or her body, starting on the trunk (stomach) and working its way around the entire body on day 4. It looks like chicken pox, but it is *not*. It does not itch. It is just a rash. Once the rash surfaces, the worst part of the virus is over. Now just wait until it goes away. There is nothing the pediatrician will give you for it. The hard part of this is, well, the baby becomes *irritable*! So much so you don't even recognize the character of your baby anymore. This can be *very* frustrating. No worries, just stick it out; it is only a week. This too shall pass, and you and your baby will be good to go.

21. Here is a trick to managing fevers that one mommy shared with me. For very high fevers that do not break, please see a pediatrician or go to the emergency room. If you try to break a mild fever at home, here is a tip: hospitals put a cold washcloth or baby wipe on a boy's testicles to break high, hard-to-break fevers. This is the alternative to those cold showers our parents used to give us. But please ask your pediatrician before doing this. Also, shower your baby frequently so he or she stays cool. Do not do a cold bath; a warm bath is better. Put some cold, wet cloths on the head and neck after a bath. Give your baby Tylenol and Motrin,

alternating of course every three hours. Motrin is a little stronger on the stomach, so make sure your baby has some food in his or her system.

22. Diaper rash is a horrible thing for both the baby and you. It is heartbreaking to see your baby with a painful and uncomfortable diaper rash. Now let's get to the bottom of this. It probably isn't a "diaper rash." Usually, there is something in the baby's diet that is causing this reaction, which is probably too much iron. When I gave birth, I was given iron pills because my iron was low. Remember, whatever you take goes to your baby when breastfeeding, so I was giving my baby too much iron in my breast milk, causing him to have a huge rash. Once I stopped the pills and put the ointment on, the rash went away. Another thing is if you are giving your baby cereal and formula, those two things have iron in them. It may be too much iron for your baby, so alternate on the cereal, feeding it maybe just once or twice a day instead of every meal. Another cause may be your baby going with a dirty diaper for too long' the acid in urine and a poopy diaper may cause irritation.. Your baby's skin may also be too sensitive for that particular diaper. Check for the first two before changing the actual diaper.

23. Earaches are no fun at all. They hurt and make babies cranky. One mommy told me that if you put a warm washcloth on your baby's ear, it will alleviate the pain. It can't hurt to try if you can't go to the doctor right away. Another thing to do is put a few drops of white vinegar in the ear that hurts or after a swim class to prevent ear infections and water in the baby's ears, which can cause a problem later if not taken care of. Another home remedy I was told for the ear was garlic and

olive oil. Garlic is a natural antibiotic and builds the immune system. Get a garlic clove and mesh it up with a little bit of olive oil, so that the garlic juice mixes with the oil. Heat it up just to be warm, put the liquid in a dropper, and put about two drops of the oil-and-garlic mixture in the ear. Put some cotton in the ear to hold the mixture in. I tried this with my baby, and it alleviated his earache. But in any situation with your child's health, please see a health- care professional.

24. Apples may constipate a baby's sensitive stomach. Bananas may or may not do the same, but that depends on your baby's stomach sensitivity. Be careful about giving your baby too much of that when feeding your baby anything, including baby food and solids. Foods that are good for constipation include prunes, pears, mango, avocado, peas and depending on your baby bananas. If your baby is in the ten- to twelve-month range, ask your doctor if constipation is a problem with your child to see if changing from full formula (if that's what you are feeding your baby) to half formula and half goat, almond, coconut, or hemp milk is possible. You are trying to figure out if the dairy in the formula is some part of the problem, even if you are giving your baby lactose-free formula.

25. Colic! This is a parent's and baby's worst nightmare! Here is a home remedy that was passed down to me. If your baby can crawl, then let him or her crawl for a while this movement helps the gas pass, this will also give you time so you can get a little bit of chamomile tea with warm water in a bottle or sippy cup. It will relax the contraction in the stomach and help soothe your baby. If you have the nighttime tea with spearmint, it will help make your baby not only calm but go

to sleep. If you have a newborn or your baby does not crawl yet you can do the motion of crawling with your baby's legs; it has the same effect. You can also rub the belly for help with relaxing the stomach muscles so they can function normally again. Place one hand on the top of the belly and the other on the bottom, retract your hands in the normal direction of your arms, and then do it again but switching placements. This also helps with the stomach muscles. Watch what you eat. (If you are breastfeeding, avoid these foods, which can cause or trigger allergic reactions in your baby or may be irritants to your baby's stomach: dairy products, eggs, cabbage family foods (broccoli), beans, coffee, spices, onions, and garlic. (This information was found on the SAFbaby website.) [1]

26. Make sure you are giving your baby a probiotic in his or her daily bottle, even with breast milk. This will help with your baby's immune system. These are healthy bacteria that will also help with digestion. Ask your pediatrician to see what brand he or she recommends and the amount of colony-forming units (CFUs) he or she prefers. The more, the better, but of course it must be appropriate for your baby's age.

27. Another insight from a mommy friend was to wear your baby in a sling or wrap your baby in a swaddle. Doing this will give off heat to your baby's stomach, which can relieve colic and gas. Prop your baby upright even while sleeping until this passes so that the pain of the gas is less because of gravity and more milk in your baby's system.

    One thing I did with my son was when I breastfed him, I made sure I was leaning against something like a pillow or

---

1 www.safbaby.com

anything I could rest on. I then latched him on but faced him down on top of me instead of facing him up toward me. This prevented the air from coming into his mouth and causing gas. Since he was facing down, he had less air and more milk in his stomach.

28. Vaccines—this is a very personal subject. You must decide what you want for your child. But I need to inform you about what happened to me and some other moms with boys at the ten- to twelve-month mark.

Now, I had my son have his vaccines one at a time. He had the Prevnar vaccine twice before his ten-month appointment. The last time, his reaction to the vaccine was for the most part normal for what they tell you is "normal" with a minor fever, irritability, sleepiness the next day, and diarrhea. What was different was that the same day I brought him home from the doctor, his meatus of the urethra (pee hole) was blood red! It did concern me, but since he didn't cry while urinating, I knew it wasn't a urinary tract infection. I put some ointment on it and waited until the next day to see if it got better, thinking it was a minor reaction or irritation of some sort like a diaper rash.

When I saw it wasn't getting better or worse, I asked a few mom friends of mine if they had had the same issue with this and if it was connected to the vaccine. These moms agreed with me and told me that their sons had the same issue after that vaccine.

I said, "But he didn't have this before," and they also said the same thing to me. Their sons didn't either. It seemed to come for all of us on the third shot. One mom even told me her son started to bleed. They said their doctor gave them some antibiotic ointment and it got better, but it took a month to go away. I was now not as freaked out, but I didn't want my son to deal with this for a month.

When I changed him again, I saw it had started to peel; a thin layer of skin from the head of the penis was peeling off. It was too late to call the doctor because of business hours so I called my primary and explained the situation. He looked it up and said that it was rare; some people had given their babies Zantac. Now I wasn't too comfortable with the Zantac idea without speaking to my pediatrician, so I skipped on that part. But my doctor said to put ointment on it and go see the doctor in the morning. Now if it was bleeding, I would have gone to the ER. Since it wasn't and was just raw skin, I protected it and did what he said.

When the pediatrician saw it, she was shocked; she had never seen that before and didn't know if there was a UTI connection between the vaccines. She said it looked burned, but since he wasn't in pain, it couldn't have been a UTI. I told her my concern. I did not want to have him go through this for a month, so she gave me two antibiotic ointments to speed up the process. I used it three times a day for five days, and he was back to normal. Thank God! So please be careful with these vaccines and watch for odd things with your baby when they are given.

29. Many babies experience a mild case of eczema due to sweat from sleep or the car seat. This is found mainly on the back or on the stomach of the baby; it's a mild discoloration or texture on the baby's skin. Once you take the baby out of the car seat or bed, wipe down the baby with a wet cloth or wipe,

and while he or she is still wet, apply coconut oil and change the shirt. You should see your baby's skin get better shortly.

30. Hiccups are both annoying to mommy and baby. If you give your little one some *gripe water* it will take the hiccups away pretty quickly. You can also help your baby by placing him/her on your lap facing down. Make sure that your baby's belly is flat on your lap then rub and tap his/her back.

31. Maintenance of genitalia is very important. There are some instances where parents are not aware of their actions or lack there of. What do I mean? For boys if they are circumcised when cleaning the penis the foreskin must be pulled back all the way and cleaned properly by wiping the head of the penis. Once the cleaning is done applying a non-petroleum gel around the head heals the circumcision area and also protects the head from the acidity from the urine. This also prevents what is most dreaded by everyone, what you may ask? If the penis is not cleaned this proper way the urine that is not cleaned creates a sticky bacteria that makes the remaining foreskin attach itself to the head of the penis not allowing the head to heal and also not giving the penis the full head and curvature it is supposed to have. This causes great pain to the baby and even as a young child. What is the outcome? The pediatrician (should do it first to show you) must pull back the foreskin so the penis may grow properly and not cause issues later on during sex. This will cause great pain to the baby and the skin that has to be pulled back may even bleed. This is not a cruel act from the pediatrician; on the contrary this is trying to help your baby not have problems in the future. If your baby boy is not circumcised then you still need to clean it properly so that the acidity in the urine

does not cause bacteria and infections. For girls, they too have foreskin over her clitoris that needs to be cleaned properly. Not as intense as the boys but still thoroughly. If you see that you baby girl is having urinary track infections even as an older child and in some cases some adults; check to see if between the foreskin of her clitoris and her clitoris is residue of wipes or toilet paper. This may occur and if not cleaned out can cause bacteria leading too a urinary track infection. Once cleaned the pain should subside. If this is not the case make sure she is drinking plenty of water and give her some cranberry juice; make sure her clothing is not tight and she uses the restroom frequently.

32. Colds and fevers, one of parents worst nightmares. Please speak to a pediatrician before using any medicines. What I have found that works is if you are giving your baby or child medicines like Tylenol or Motrin they must be age appropriate (they do have infant which is best for babies) the regular dose is every four hours., but if you use both of them you can alternate from Tylenol and Motrin every two hours. This also works when your child is teething. Please ask your pediatrician before doing this though. There are also homeopathic medicines for babies from up to two months of age; just ask your pharmacist for assistance. There is also a homeopathic vitamin C tablets that dissolve with water or saliva that may boost your child's immune system as well as organic baby elderberry. When you put your baby to sleep make sure they have a humidifier close by to loosen up congestion and help relieve coughs. Applying a small amount of baby Vicks on the bottom of your baby's feet and covering it up with socks will help with this as well. Please

follow proper instructions on any medications even Vicks. The wall adaptors for Vicks also help your baby sleep and breathe better. Another item to use is saline. If you use saline up the nose and squirt a little bit in the mouth will break up congestion in the sinuses as well as in the chest.

33. Night terrors, another name for nightmares for babies. This is when your baby is sleeping and all of a sudden you hear your baby cry or scream; your heart starts to race as you go check on your little to see they are still sleeping; and possibly still crying. What do you do? Well it's not good to just pick up your baby in a rush or scared while he/she is sleeping. This will wake him/her up in a bigger scare than he/she already is. This is a horrible thought to think your little one that hopefully hasn't had a bad or traumatic experience yet; have such a bad dream. How is that possible? It could be as simple as you leaving, a toy being taken, a scolding, anything they may not like. All you need to do is gently and lovingly caress your baby and softly shush and say "mommy's or daddy's here its okay" once your baby wakes up and cries then you can pick them up calmly and calm your baby down. You can try rocking, feeding a bottle/breastfeed, singing, hugging and caressing; all of these actions may calm your baby. Once your baby is calm just assure him/her "its just a dream its okay". Once you feel comfortable that your baby is calm and ready then place them back into bed to go to sleep.

34. Rolling over is an achievement for little babies, though for a mom is a bit nerve wrecking. This usually occurs at the four to five month mark. Though a baby can roll over it's a bit more difficult to roll back. This step comes a little later after a baby rolls over; be aware that once your little one learns

to roll over sleeping may be a bit different. Sleeping on the stomach becomes a favorite position for little babies at this stage. At this point mom starts to freak out because of the scare of SIDS. Please remain calm and just watch your baby, learn to let go a little and trust them. If you are still swaddling you do not have to worry as much. But if you are not then just keep an eye on your baby. Know this, most babies that have built the stomach muscles to roll over because of tummy time have also built back muscles to protect themselves from suffocation. Though they may not be able to roll back they are still able to lift up their head incase they vomit or spit up and change positions, this should calm mommy's nerves a bit when your baby is sleeping. SIDS usually happens most before the baby learns to hold up his/her head and roll over. Soon after your baby starts to roll over and hold his/her head up you will see your little baby magically moves from one side of the crib to the other and you have no idea how. This is all because of those stomach and back muscles they are learning to use and move around.

First Few Months

Congratulations! You have made it through pregnancy, you made it through birth, and now all you need to do is make it through your first year! If you are a single dad who has lost his wife during birth, my condolences go out to you. You deserve a medal for taking on this responsibility on your own. It is much harder for a man to do this on his own (normally) than it is for a woman. (Due to motherly instincts, it just comes naturally to most moms anyway.) This is the hardest year for a child and a new parent. For this reason, I am writing this book for all new parents and parents-to-be. Let's make this joyous yet difficult journey just a little bit easier to deal with.

A child is the biggest blessing anyone can ever have, and to be honest, my son is the best masterpiece that I ever created; just the blessing alone to create a human being is an honor. But putting that aside, it is also the hardest job anyone could ever do. Though a child brings joy to a home, he or she also brings *a lot* of hardship and stress, especially between the parents. Studies have shown that because of the stress of a child, marriages tend to split within the first year of a baby's life. Let's try to bring that number down and find ways to help Mommy and Daddy survive the first year.

I know you would think, *But it's a baby. How hard can that be? Why would that break up a marriage?* Well, parents are sleep-deprived and stressed out because of the grueling workload a new baby requires. If you have no sleep and have to function perfectly, it is very hard to deal with even for one day. So try, oh, say, four months of that at least. It is stressful, but not impossible, even though you may feel like it is when you're in the moment.

Before the baby arrives, sit down with your partner and talk about what needs to be done around the house. List the chores that need to be done, and split them up to what you think you can do. Now, remember, moms, you will have your hands full for the majority of the time with the newborn baby, so let Daddy take care of the majority of the stuff for the first three months until the worst part is over. Then things can shift around to what you can do with the baby. If you can, try to get a third party to help you with household chores, like cooking, laundry, and so on. You will need it. Maybe ask your mom, mother-in-law, aunt, friend, or anyone who is willing to help out. Remember, both of you will be tired and cranky, so extra help will be necessary.

Now, I have made this list for my household because of this very issue. The distribution of chores and responsibilities can cause some issues if both parties are not on the same page. Now, ladies, no matter how great your husband can be, the majority of the responsibility will fall on your lap in a regular situation. Why? Well, because we can handle more stress and responsibility anyway, or at least most women can. You are a superhuman, and the stronger sex. Do you question it? If you do, well, just look down at your bump. Mommy is the only person who can do this. Your mommy gear will kick in once your baby arrives, and you become Superwoman! Dads, on the other hand (unless they are single dads at the newborn stage and have no choice), well, they just don't do it as easily as women for the most part anyway. They grow as the baby grows. What do I mean by that? They develop a lot slower than you do (normally).

This may not be true for all men, but the majority fall into this category. If you have an exceptional man who does not need this list or need to be told what to do or be watched while with the baby, then you are one blessed woman! He is a keeper, so cherish each other—not that you shouldn't anyway, but just a little more because he is so special.

Now, this is the list my husband and I came up with just to relieve the stress and share responsibilities. He works from home and tends to clients and appointments, and I have stayed at home with our son. Please feel free to use this and modify it to your household and what works for you all. I hope this helps out like it has in my house and makes parenting a little bit easier. Now if you have a nanny who can do all the major stuff for you, *great!* But if you do not, let's work things out, shall we? This is for the mom who stays at home; if you work, then the chores may differ, especially if there is help at home. The times for baby care depend on the time your baby sleeps, and that changes every three months until about the time your baby sleeps through the night. Then it is easier for the parents to get their rest so they are not so sleep deprived.

THE LIST

Mommy	Daddy

BABY Care
* Once baby sleeps through the night
7AM-7PM (whenever daddy is done working from 5-7pm)
 	
Night Shift: Every other night
Diapers/Bottles During Shifts
Tend to Baby when sick
* Research and Attend to:
 	
  Baby Productivity
  Development & Pictures
  Baby Activities
  Baby Education
  Baby Doctor Visits
	BABY Care
	
	7PM (or when is done working from 5-7PM) Bath Nightly
	
	Night Shift: Every other night
	Diapers/Bottles During Shifts
	
	Tend to Baby when sick
	  Baby Doctor Visits
	
	* *For Newborns this sleep schedule does not apply. What worked for us was nightly*
	
	  Mommy: 10PM-2AM
	  Daddy: 2AM-6AM

Daily/Weekly Chores:
 	
Daily: Dinner
 	
Weekly/Bi Weekly: Buy Groceries
 	
Baby Chores:
  Laundry (Mommy & Baby)
  Cut Baby's Nails
  Buy Baby Supplies
 	
Household:
 	
* Maintain house upkeep
* Buy any household necessity
* Buy any necessity for household members
* Buy any gifts needed for any occasion for all family members.
	Daily/Weekly Chores:
	
	Daily: Dishes & Bottles Cleaned Nightly
	Trash Emptied
	
	Dogs Cared For: Walked/Food/Water/
	Grooming
	
	Weekly: Laundry (own)
	Put Up Groceries **(The day bought)**
	Dry Cleaning
	Put Up Baby Supplies **(The day bought)**
	Anything on the TO DO LIST involving to build or put away heavy items

* Deal with, Schedule and Attend any issues involving **Utilities ex.**
    Internet/Cable
    Water
    Health Insurance for family
    House Cleaning Maid
    Maintenance of house
 * Event Planning for travel, parties or any other occasion. Also any task needed with that including organizing, invitations and research.
 * Tend to house décor or projects needed.
	Monthly: Pay Bills

Weekends
 	
 Saturday: Date Night 8PM
    When available
 	
 Sunday: OPTIONS:
    Church & Lunch
    Parks
    Walks
    Shopping
    Beach (if available)
    BBQ with Family/Friends
    Family Functions & Birthdays
	Weekends:
	 Saturday:
	    Work only if necessary.
	    Date Night 8PM When available
	 Sunday: OPTIONS:
	    Church & Lunch
	    Parks
	    Walks
	    Shopping
	    Beach (if available)
	    BBQ with Family/Friends
	    Family Functions & Birthdays

Now that we have covered chores for Mommy and Daddy when the baby arrives, let's talk about what it is like when the baby does arrive. What is it like to have a baby for the first few days? Well, to begin with, it is very overwhelming and joyous and scary all at the same time. You are now in charge of a human being who totally depends on you to live. *No pressure!* It is also very exhausting because of the lack of sleep. But to give you an idea what the schedule comes out to be, I have a picture of my son's schedule for the first four days at the hospital, which did not change when he was at home.

The chart on the next page will give you an idea of what a full schedule normally looks like. Don't be deceived this is feeding, burping and diaper change, this normally lasts about an hour to an hour and a half to do this process. You may only have about twenty to thirty minutes of rest time in between feedings.

AuG 29th, 2015

TIME:	DAY 1 FEEDING	WET DIAPER	DIRTY DIAPER	DAY 2 FEEDING	WET DIAPER	DIRTY DIAPER	DAY 3 FEEDING	WET DIAPER	DIRTY DIAPER	DAY 4 FEEDING	WET DIAPER	DIRTY DIAPER
12:00AM												
1:00AM										1:50✓	✓	✓
2:00AM				✓2:10			1:45✓					
3:00AM						2:40✓	3:20✓			3:10✓	✓	
4:00AM						3:10				3:40		
5:00AM							5:20✓					
6:00AM										6:15✓	✓	✓
7:00AM												
8:00AM							8:15✓	✓	✓	9:15✓	✓	
9:00AM												
10:00AM				10:30am ✓	✓30	11:30	10:15✓		✓	10:30✓	✓	✓
11:00AM				✓	11		✓10am	✓	✓	11:25		
12:00PM				12✓	12:30✓		12:40✓		✓			
1:00PM				1:45✓	1:40✓		1:50					
2:00PM				2:50✓								
3:00PM												
4:00PM	4:30✓	✓	✓	4:00✓			4:35					
5:00PM		5:00✓	✓		5:00✓		5:45✓	✓	5:40✓			
6:00PM			✓	6:05✓					6:35✓			
7:00PM							7:00✓					
8:00PM	8:15✓	8:15✓	✓	9:30✓			8:20✓	✓				
9:00PM							9:05✓	✓	✓10			
10:00PM	10:45✓	✓	✓	10:20✓			10:25✓					
11:00PM	11:00✓	✓	✓11:00✓				11:05am✓					

I hope this gives you an idea of what your new schedule will be like with the baby so you can adjust to it more easily and plan your household around it. It is also a good idea for you to keep track of all feedings and diaper changes for your doctor visits; they will ask you about it.

If you have pets, please make arrangements for someone other than Mommy to take care of them. I did so indefinitely; they are now my husband's responsibility because I'm always dealing with the baby.

Please remember you both will be exhausted and you will forget things and be very irritable. You also have a new life to care for so please have that at the top of your mind. Do not forget to *communicate*.

I say this in italics because it is *so important* to talk about everything and how you feel about things so you can both understand each other and make things work with less stress and fewer arguments. Come to an agreement on rules, chores, and people who will visit and when they visit. This is key to keep your sanity and home less stressful. Mommy and the baby need their rest.

I have also learned that whatever stress Mommy has is fed to the baby in energy and can make him or her cranky and irritable. It also changes the taste of the breast milk if you are breastfeeding. So try to keep calm through the storm because this too shall pass. If you don't have any help, at least order a delivery service with the food of your liking for at least the first month or two. This will help out tremendously.

Try to take shifts when possible; if you are breastfeeding, this will be a little harder to do because you are the source of food. If you can have your partner alternate nights or time slots to care for the baby while Mommy sleeps or, if he works from home, have him take the baby for a bit in the morning so that you can sleep, this will be of great help.

Don't worry about a schedule right away. Remember, this is all new to the baby and his or her schedule is off. He or she has no regulation of day or night. Your baby will eventually create his or her own schedule for sleep and feeding around three months or so. If you need to set it because you have to return to work, then try to do so around this time too, so the baby can get adjusted to his or her new world and you to your baby. Try to take things one day at a time and one thing at a time. You will notice your life has just slowed down to a snail's pace. If you live life in the fast lane, well, this will change all of that and will give you time to stop and smell the roses.

Life as a new mom, especially for the first three to four months, can be very slow and frustrating if you are usually in the fast lane, but you have to realize your life has just changed and you need to go at a different pace. For example, if you managed to eat something at least by 2:00 p.m., you have done something good. If you took a shower today and got dressed, you had a fantastic day! Am I joking? *No*! This is for real. If you didn't get to take a shower one day and got to take one the next day, you still are doing well. You have to let it all be okay. Remember, this too shall pass. You just had a very productive day in your new life.

When you try to leave the house for a doctor visit or for any reason, you need to start getting ready at least four hours in advance. Why? Well, you have to feed, change, probably feed again, and do another diaper change after that. Then, you need to change the baby into some clothes, and don't forget the nap time. You never want to wake up a baby from a nap or deprive a baby of a nap. If you do, you will have one cranky, upset baby, and when you are so exhausted and sleep deprived, you can't afford to deal with that.

Then, you have the opportunity to get yourself ready and take a shower, get dressed into something other than pajamas, and feel human again as well as eat something probably for the first time in that day. Then, when the baby wakes up, you will have to go through that entire process again. Don't forget the diaper bag needs to be packed with plenty of diapers, two to three changes of clothes for the baby, bibs, burp rags, and formula, if you are using it. Then, you somehow have to manage to get out of the house and to your appointment. Maybe this time, the nap will be in the car during the ride to your destination. Make sure you cover up because you will get spit up on and will have to change your shirt or outfit. Just remember to breathe, and everything will be okay. If you get this one thing done all day, you had a very productive day. Give this about four months or so, and this too shall pass and get easier to deal with.

For a new mom who is usually very active, this can get frustrating. You are used to doing things quickly and for yourself, and now you see yourself barely doing anything at all and being a slave driven by a newborn baby. How could this be? Motherly instinct, now you only think about your baby and your baby's needs before your own. Welcome to motherhood! This will be your new way of life and way of being, and you cannot help but to be this way. You love your baby more than this world, and it is the only thing to do and way to be. Get used to it, and put on a happy face. Cry at home when needed.

I know I cried and frankly still do. Yeah, Mom, you do all the dirty work, fact of life! You spend all day with the baby if you stay at home. If you have a nanny or go to work, then life is a little different but still the majority of the responsibility is on your shoulders. Sucks, doesn't it? This is true unless you have a rare breed of husband who is a super dad and helps out in the house and takes care of the baby not just by playing with him or her for thirty minutes and handing the baby over to you when he is done; if you have the super dad who actually parents the baby, then please from all mothers give him the father of the year award and care for each other! This is priceless and very rare!

Most fathers do not understand what it takes to care for a baby, much less a newborn while being sleep deprived. They go off to work, especially in your first months, and live their lives as normal. You, on the other hand, do not. You slave over your new bundle of joy, barely able to think straight. You are so tired and hungry and achy that you are on automatic, neglecting yourself as a woman and person while forgetting your own needs because you are busy with the baby's needs. Finally, in the late afternoon, you are lucky enough to brush your teeth, and your husband walks in and looks around at a mess in the house and says, "What have you done all day?"

What! is what you feel inside, and you want to jump at him and throw him against a wall like a character from *The Matrix*, wringing his neck and saying, "Why don't you try this?"

In your mind, you are racing through all the things you had to overcome, all the stress with a newborn, the crying and tears, the sleep deprivation, and the body ache, trying to recover from your delivery as well as working through this occurrence called breast engorgement, and God forbid your baby gets sick with a cold or something and is cranky. OMG! Let's not forget you are more exhausted than you have ever been in your life and with all your postpartum hormones, you are so dearly emotionally sensitive, much more than you have been in your entire life of emotional imbalance due to your monthly period.

This *is* the hardest thing you will ever do in your life, and you have to do it all with no sleep. I know when people talk about being sleep deprived, it's unfamiliar to you or not understandable until you have lived this catastrophic period. You barely had time to relax, and he says, "What did you do all day?" expecting the house to be cleaned and dinner cooked and ready for him. Um ... *no*! Here is where the ground rules need to be laid out, and trust me, ladies, it won't be easy.

I know of women who have done drastic things like leaving the house for a day or even the weekend, leaving the baby with their husbands to "figure it out" and appreciate what they do at home with the little one all day and how much of themselves that they have to give up. When you bring a baby into this world; that is when you realize who your husband really is and vice versa. Why? Because that is when responsibility hits him and he can't get out. He is no longer a bachelor or a husband with a wife who can take care of herself. Now he is a father with a load of bricks that has fallen on his shoulders. Some dads can handle it right away, but for some, it takes a few scary head bumps to deal with it, especially those men who have never had to deal with anything or anyone before. Now, I'm not here to man-bash; I'm here to give you a reality check so that you can be aware of the things that happen to all women when a baby arrives. I hope you can prevent this or at least take it in a little better when it happens, because it will.

As you and your baby grow together, life gets a little bit "easier" one day at a time. After the three-month mark, you get used to your new life and you are able to handle it better. This is why we say, "It gets easier." It really doesn't; you see, you just get used to it and are able to deal with it. Then every three months, your baby goes through a new phase of ability and life, and Mommy adjusts to the changes. The more independent the baby gets, the less newborn work that Mommy does. Then starts the new challenges that any growing child goes through. Though you still won't have the time to sit and read a book, you will find time to possibly clean the kitchen or a room or do laundry. Maybe! You may not have time to fold it or put it away, but at least it's clean!

Now let's talk about some changes within Mommy once the baby has arrived. Your belly will not be flat, but it will go away quickly if you breastfeed and when you heal if you exercise and eat healthily. Embrace it, and try not to criticize it too much. I mean, you did just make a human and got it out of your body. Give it some time to recuperate. One thing that did happen to me was that I had very vivid nightmares about my baby's safety. What could I do better to protect him and how safe was he really? It made me lose more sleep than I was already.

This occurred for a while because I was under a lot of stress. Once that stress was relieved, the dreams started to diminish until they were completely gone. Moms also go through anxiety and sleep training. Your baby finally sleeps through the night, and you find yourself not sleeping through the night. *Why*? Remember that you have trained yourself to wake up every two hours or so depending on whatever your baby's schedule was. Your body is now used to that, and you have to retrain it to go back to the way it was, sleeping through the night. Try meditation to help you. And depression—just because it is called depression doesn't mean it really is the traditional meaning of depression. You don't have to be depressed to be depressed. Tricky, huh? Your body has gone through a lot of changes, and postpartum depression brings anxiety and sleep deprivation. Try seeing a psychiatrist to help you out with this common situation so you get better sleep.

Still to this day, I get teary-eyed when I talk about my son and something special or sentimental; this has to do with baby blues. Your emotions are exaggerated, and you become sensitive. This is totally normal; after all, you just departed from your baby, who was inside you for nine months. Your hormones are still a little bit out of whack. So if you find yourself crying for no reason or being extra sensitive, it's okay.

Like I said before, mothers change three times in their lives, and now you have just changed again after changing nine months ago. It can also be very stressful to figure out who you are and what kind of a mother you are or have become. Try not to lose yourself too much; keep the old you too. Some women get more protective, and some get more laid back; either way, give yourself some time to figure out who you have become and learn to deal with it and adjust to the new you. Figure out what you will and will not tolerate for your baby and from your baby so that you may parent your child how you want to.

Physical enjoyment and sexual interaction with your partner may also take a turn. Of course, this varies with every woman. Some women have a high sexual desire after the baby is born and want to be intimate like they were before baby with their partners. Others do not. Seems odd? Not really, if you think about it. It may not have to do directly with your partner; it has to do with you, Mom. You spent ten months (forty weeks or so) creating this beautiful human being. After your entire life, your body, which was once yours, now has become food grounds, nurturing and comforting someone else. The last thing that you want after spending all day with someone sucking on your breasts for food is to come to an intimate night. When your partner approaches you to stimulate your breasts, really, the last thing you want to feel is more sucking! You may just be turned off, and your intimate life may be nonexistent for a while until you transition with your baby.

Breastfeeding

Now, let's talk about this for a brief moment. If you do not wish to breastfeed, you may skip this section and move on to the next one. If you choose to do this, well, brace yourself. Now, like with everything in this book, I keep saying everyone is different and experiences different things. Some mothers may experience some things and not others. But one thing is for sure! Breastfeeding is *not easy*! It's awkward for you and for the baby because it's a first for the both of you. Maybe it's not and you forgot. At the end of the day, it ends up being hard. Some babies latch on really well and do minimal damage to Mommy, which is a fantastic gift. If not, then, well, join the club.

Breastfeeding hurt me so badly my toes curled when my baby cried for milk, tears came down my face, and I clenched my jaw shut so I wouldn't scream. I also had to control myself while holding his head so as not to hurt him because to me it was so painful. I mean imagine your soft, beautiful nipples that are so tender and have never gone through anything traumatic because of the protection of the bra now having the life sucked out of them and extracting milk. Trust me; men have *nothing* on babies going for some food.

My experience was unbelievably painful. I got blisters, and I bled. I had to put cooling pads on them. I tried pumping just so he didn't have to latch on to me and keep hurting me, but even that was just a little bit of milk that would come out and not enough for the baby—nothing like the actual latch for feeding. I even got a fever and pain in my breasts, which is called engorgement. I had to jump in the hot shower and massage my breasts so they would loosen up all the clogged milk, while holding my tongue from the pain breathing in and out to try to relax myself through the process. At the end I gave into latching on my baby and he made the engorgement go away. There is no suction like a baby. Now, some women do not go through this, and that is great, but if you do go through this, just hold it out and stick it through the *first four weeks*. That is when your body builds its callus on your nipples, and then it becomes a breeze and second nature. It's the best thing you can do for your baby.

Sleep Training

After a few months of sleep deprivation a mother's desire is to sleep through the night. Not only does she crave a good nights sleep for herself but for her baby as well. At least that is what I have learned from my own experience as well as some other mothers I know. Though some mothers found it hard to sleep train their baby. Since I am a sleeper, being sleep deprived was not on my top favorite list since early on. I knew once my baby was born that I was determined to have him sleep trained very quickly.

I researched the internet and spoke to other mothers and my therapist, I found out a few tricks and put them all together and *poof* my son was sleep trained at four months old sleeping through the entire night of twelve hours of sleep plus three naps a day. *Whew,* coming from a baby that only gave me twenty minutes of nap time at a time and didn't give me much time for anything really- to one hour and a half three times a day of nap time and twelve hours a night of sleep. I am so thankful to God for giving me this gift! I transitioned my son to his crib at two and a half months because I did not want to be stuck having to sleep with him so early or having my baby stay up late. I wanted him to know he had his room and his bed and that is his place to sleep. Once I found the trick this task was easy.

I just knew that if I did not find a solution to my problem I was going to be one mean mommy. That is not what I wanted to for the sake of my sanity and health I made it my mission to find a solution. Well after much research I found what worked for my son and I was for the first few months that he was still little was the 5 S's that I mentioned earlier on the tips section from *the Happiest Baby on the Block book*. This worked like a charm, though for some moms they claim that it did not work for them. The thing is that with the 5 S's it has to be done when your baby is a new born. I would say from birth till about five to six months old, the steps has to be done exactly right or it will not work.

What happens after the six months? Well this is when you transfer over to the nighttime routine of a book, song whatever you do and then lights out a kiss goodnight and what I call the magic box. A noise machine will work wonders, it will make your baby sleep just a little bit longer because he/she will not be hearing the outside noises to wake him/her up. What the baby hears is the wave sound or whatever sound you choose that is calming to listen to all night long. So if you have a noisy dog next door, or loud neighbors that will not longer be a problem with a noise machine.

If your baby cries just soothe your baby and say "its okay, its bedtime goodnight" and walk away. Close the door behind you and watch through your monitor what your baby does. Yes the crying may continue a bit, but it will soon be over and your baby will get over it and play a little in the crib before falling asleep on his or her own. This is a way they learn to self soothe. Now I'm not saying to do the cry out method because that becomes traumatizing later in life with abandonment issues. At least in my belief, the shushing works; if you see your baby still crying but tantrum style then after a few minutes go back into the room and put your baby down in the bed without taking them out of the crib. Repeat what you said earlier "its okay, its bedtime goodnight" shush your baby a bit and walk away again.

If the crying still continues after a few more minutes say three to five minutes then this time just open the door and again repeat shushing and "its okay, its bedtime goodnight" shush again and close the door. This allows your baby to know you are there as a support in this transition without abandonment, but they need to learn how to self soothe themselves to sleep. Keep reminding yourself this is a process that needs repetition and sooner than later you will see bedtime will be a breeze and anyone will be able to put your baby to sleep. This leaves you with date night and your partner helping out with bedtime as well.

Now there is more to this sleeping through the night process than just what steps to take on putting your baby down to sleep. It also means that the last bottle of the night must be the *last bottle of the night*. What if you breastfeed? Well breastfeeding only moms if you want to sleep train you must give up the last bottle to formula. Why? Well breast milk is water based and does not hold much substance; this is why your baby wakes up at night because of hunger. Yes stick it out for the first four months but after that if you want to sleep the last bottle should be at least fifty percent formula. I did this and also added a quarter of a baby spoonful of cereal. This fill's up your baby's belly and he/she can hold on until morning. If you do not do this type of training then you just created a bad habit for your baby. Your baby will know that in the middle of the night he/she will get fed, so he/she will wake up wanting milk. But if you give your baby formula at night and rinse your baby's mouth after that milk bottle with water to take away any film left over to clean the mouth. (This can be a routine until your baby starts to have teeth and you can then brush your baby's teeth.) This process will be a cue that this is the last feeding until morning. When your baby cries, shush him/her from the door and let him/her soothe him or herself back to sleep. Once you do this a few nights in a row your baby will get used to not eating at night and you have successfully trained your baby to sleep perfectly throughout the night. Now you can finally rest and enjoy your evening.

Men

We have been talking a lot about the mom and what she is going through, what will happen and how to take care of the baby. There is another part of this equation, though, and it is Daddy, the man who helped create this bundle of love. What is he going through? If you haven't had him read this book yet, now would be a good time to at least have him listen to you read it or have him read it with you. I say together so you both understand what goes on from a third party. I find that when someone else who is not in the relationship tells you something, you take it into consideration better and are willing to listen.

Okay, are we ready? Listen up, couples; this is the most crucial point in this book. Why? Well, because if this part doesn't work—and I mean the connection and communication between you two—then your marriage will be in limbo and possibly fall into the statistics and end in a divorce. We do not want that, do we? I didn't think so.

When a woman finds out she is expecting, from one split moment to the other, her mind completely changes and she begins to think about what she must do or change to make this person inside her grow properly and make it to birth. This is milestone #1; milestone #2 is after a successful birth, becoming parents and having the baby survive his or her first year. Yay! A lot of things happen to Mom, physical, mental, and emotional, within those two years. But what about Dad?

Dad all of a sudden goes from a husband thinking about himself and his wife predominately to being a creator of a life that depends on him as a provider and an example. If you are a single dad or mom with a baby, then this part also happens to you and you get a double whammy! Dad's mind also does a shift from one moment to another, from, *Cool, we're doing well as a couple!* to *Money, money, money!* He sees the baby as a bottomless pit of money-sucking. He is pretty much right! While Mommy worries about how to stay healthy and eat right, Daddy worries about how to pay the bills. *(This is not the case in a lot of homes that both parents work; this is a generalization.)*

This first shift for a couple can be pretty hard to deal with if both parties don't understand what the other is going through. He needs to make the family survive in one way, and she needs to make herself and the baby survive in another way. His worries are financial and very valid, *but* Dad cannot forget that Mom-to-be needs his attention as well. This is a very exciting time with the new news, and Mom-to-be needs to share this special moment with the very person who helped create it. So as overwhelming as all this is for Dad financially, he just needs to take it one day at a time and one thing at a time. Dad, from every paycheck, save as much as you can and set it aside for the baby. What I mean is wait until you get the stuff you want from your baby shower and then use the money you've been saving all this time to get everything else you need (usually at the seven-month mark so

Mommy still feels good and can still move around to prepare for the baby's arrival.)This way, you are not so stressed.

Now do not be cheap and not go out with your wife because of this. You need to balance things out because both of you need to enjoy this time together, just the two of you before the baby arrives. Once this baby arrives, things will *never be the same*! Going out will not be as easy unless you have a nanny all the time or can afford a sitter or your parents are willing to give up their weekend to babysit. If you do, then that's great for you and your relationship. If not, well, enjoy it through pregnancy because you will miss it once the baby comes.

Now, Dad, remember Mom-to-be is going through some really funky stuff with hormones, physical changes, sleep deprivation, and a lot of uncomfortable body stuff. Your part in this is to be understanding to her even though you do not understand what she is going through. Let her talk to you about it, or ask her how she is and if you can do anything for her. Really, a back rub or foot rub will help her tons! Some moms can handle a nice warm bubble bath with lit candles every once in a while.

This is even truer during the last trimester because the weight of the baby puts strains on Mom's changing body. Give her a treat; it will put her in a better mood. Help Mom with eating healthy; do not shove the fact that you can drink alcohol and she can't in her face.

On the plus side, Mom-to-be has raging hormones that can work to your benefit. She becomes more sexual, and you become lucky.

Now that your wife is pregnant, she should stay away from cleaning the house because of the harmful chemicals in cleaning products, so make arrangements for someone else, either you, a relative, or a cleaning service, to come every two weeks to tend to your home.

Okay, let's talk about when baby arrives. This is crucial! As much as you love this new person—more than anyone can believe until that day arrives—you, Dad, have to man the fort for a while. What do I mean? Well, Mom has just had a traumatic experience with her body, and she and the baby need to recuperate. Dad needs to man the house and work and help with the baby. If you haven't done so before, it is crucial now for recovery after birth that someone else other than Mom cleans the house biweekly. If you do not know how to cook, have someone bring you food or cook for you or order a cantina (this is a preselected menu from a restaurant that will automatically deliver to your house on certain days or time of day daily) for at least six to eight weeks. Trust me; you will be so tired after the baby comes because of lack of sleep the last thing you will want to do is cook and clean.

Just after the baby arrives is not the time to be entertaining guests or relatives from out of town especially if they want to stay in your home. If these relatives are to visit, it is best to have them stay at a near by hotel. This will make mom, baby and even dad a little bit more at ease during this transition. Don't do too much. Remember, Mom is going to be recovering from a traumatic physical, mental, and emotional experience. Maybe a few well-wishers who are healthy and helpful are fine, but do not add extra stress on yourself when there is no need.

Visitors who can't help out with the necessities waste precious time and energy and create stress. They can even bring germs into your home. At the beginning, it is the perfect time to be overprotective about your little one who just entered this world. What better reason to be protective than your baby's health, no matter what others say. Now, don't be rude about it; be polite, but state what your wishes are. People must respect them at this time. Once the first three months is over and everyone has recuperated, make arrangements that if someone comes to see the baby and your wife, he or she must help out. One person can come and watch the baby while Mom gets to shower and have something to eat. Another can come to see the baby and help with laundry or feeding. This will alleviate stress from Mom and Dad and be more of a pleasant experience for everyone. If no one can help do this, Dad, I'm sorry, but you're going to have to for the first two months until Mom recovers. This is also a lot of workload for Dad to all of a sudden encounter and can be overwhelming for him to deal with. But who said having a baby was easy? It is hard work for both parents. Some dads handle it better than others. If you have a good dad who can take this on without complaints, Mom, you have the dad of the year! Do something to show your appreciation. Oh and one more thing, Dad, FYI the number-one job of a dad to help mom after all day with the baby is to wash bottles every night (if you are using them).

Now do not think that just because you are doing more of the work around the house and your own job that you get off the hook from night duties. You don't! Why? Because Mom has to do it all day and she is very sleep deprived, she will need help at night at least in changing the diapers. The getting up and down while she is recovering can cause serious issues and pain especially if she had a C-section. Besides, it will help you bond with your baby in a different way since Mom has to be doing the majority of the work with the baby and building her strong bond with him or her. Help at night and maybe even a bath; or so that will build a special bond between you and your little one; since babies don't really play just yet.

This will be a very sexy point in your wife's eyes, and she will thank you and praise you for it. There is nothing sexier than a dad taking care of his baby. Now if you are reluctant and cause problems because you do not want to help out or are tired, just remember you will *never be as tired as Mom.*

Remember, Dad, while you go about your daily life as normal as possible, your wife is home dealing with her body's issues, such as leaking breasts, sore and bleeding nipples, an extra thirty-plus pounds (because she is no longer pregnant and now it's just baby fat, something she is not used too), and an outraged little person screaming at her all day long—all of this after not sleeping and little to no training. She will also be dealing with breastfeeding, which is another ordeal in itself.

So be kind and understanding to her no matter what you think you are going through. She needs your support, as well as your tenderness and attention, now more than ever. Help her out with the baby; give her a break to rest or go out without the baby. This is the type of child support she needs. If you do not, your marriage *will* suffer. Mom will think you do not love her or the baby if this behavior occurs or continues. If that is the case, your marriage will diminish and you will become a statistic and end up in a divorce. So since we are trying to prevent this from happening, please understand your part and role as the fantastic husband and father you are. Duty calls!

Now, Mom, I'm going to talk to you with Dad. Let him be a part of your little one's life. Do not be domineering or demanding. Let him be his way with the baby, though safely. Obviously, do not let him abuse or hurt the baby. Remember, he is learning too. Both of you are learning how to be parents and also discovering who your baby is.

Involve Dad in the baby's life so they have a relationship too and Dad feels like he has his new connection with the baby just like you have yours. Don't shut him out because you feel he doesn't know what to do. You are probably right, and he doesn't know what to do, but you need to teach him how to do things and listen to him when he comes up with an idea. Sometimes, it may just be better than yours. This will give you a break from the baby to relax or do something you need to do.

Babies know there is a difference between Mom's care and Dad's care, and they can and will adapt to it. It is okay! Dads give the baby what moms can't because moms are so caring and careful. Dads roughhouse the baby. It's like crack to them, and they love it! So embrace it. If you have to, look away and let them be and bond. Now of course always keep an eye out just in case.

Let's talk about sex (or no sex). Dad, I know you have not been with your wife since the baby was born or before because of circumstances and recovery, but remember that list I gave you that Mommy is going through while you are at work? Well, that does not make her feel sexy or desirable, no matter what you may tell her. After all that, sex may be the *last* thing on her mind. Be patient with her. After all, she is the one going through all these changes, which are very difficult to deal with.

I want to briefly talk about depression after the baby arrives. Dad, please watch over Mommy. These signs may be subtle or more obvious and need to be taken care of. Sometimes, moms do not realize it, so dads need to jump in and be observant of mom's behavior and interactions in life and with the baby. Watch out for her in her dreams, thoughts, and excessive crying. Crying after a baby is normal but not to excess. Thoughts of hurting herself or the baby—or anyone for that matter—are serious signs of postpartum depression. Milder signs are spoken about earlier in the book. Please call to get help from a doctor or therapist. Mommy deserves her baby and loves her baby and family. She needs to be happy and healthy but mostly understand that she is not alone and she has the help and support she needs to get through this rough time.

Vaccines

What are we really putting into our children? Do we know? I mean *really* know? Or are we just following the rules? Most people think they *must* put vaccines into their children because they have to if they want them to go to school. Other people believe in them for protection against viruses. But do we really know what is going on and what is put in these vaccines?

I had no idea about this; all I knew was that they had side effects of fever, diarrhea, runny nose, excessive sleeping, irritability, changes in behavior, swelling and redness of the injected area. My entire life I was led to believe this was a "normal reaction" to the vaccine. Why is that normal? None of this is normal. Our parents didn't know the difference, but now I'm here to open your eyes. It is definitely too late for us but not for our babies and children. The vaccines now are much different than they were in our generation, with a lot more toxin ingredients. If you have already given your baby or child vaccines, well, what is done is done. Hopefully there has not been any triggers or side effects that has caused your baby or child to change. Either health wise or signs like ADHD or autism, etcetera.

I must admit I did start my son on some of the vaccines, but now that I am aware of what is in them, he will never get one again! How will I do that? Well, there are places in your city where you can go to do this. It is a religious exemption from immunization form. Go to an immunization clinic and tell them you want this form. They will ask you questions and tell you all the terrible things that can happen to a child who is not vaccinated; just say, "I am aware, and due to my religion, I do not wish for my child to be vaccinated." I say this in advance before you see the ingredients. Try to see a holistic pediatrician in your area to care for your child. You only get one opportunity in each child's life to do this if you choose to. Make sure you get three copies of this form, one for your keeping, one for your pediatrician, and one for the school or day care.

What do you do to maintain a healthy child with no immunizations? Keeping a healthy diet is crucial, especially now with all the GMOs, hormones, pesticides, and antibiotics put into foods—and the mystery meat we get at a convenient fast-food restaurant. If you believe in chiropractic care, go get adjusted to keep your spine in line so it boosts your immunity and you stay healthy. If you need a reference or information about this, go to www.grovechiropractic.com; if you are in the area, they may be able to help you. If not, go to a chiropractor who does the same thing.

Another good source of knowledge is www.thegreatergood.org. There is a video clip there to order, it will show you a lot more information about vaccines and different scenarios, and you can make your decision then. I hope you find this research helpful for the health of your children. If we share knowledge, then our eyes are open and we are able to make healthy decisions on our own instead of just following the rules.

My husband's friend has a little girl, and one day, he took her in for a regular vaccine. She was a normal, healthy little girl. When she got the vaccine (it will stay anonymous), within twenty-four hours, he saw his precious little girl change right in front of him to a child with autism. Now I'm not saying that vaccines cause autism. What I am saying is that if your child has a gene that can be triggered by a certain chemical or ingredient in a vaccine; that can cause the child's genetic makeup to change and him or her to turn autistic or have ADHD or anything else that may be worse.

The problem is that you don't know until it's too late. It is really up to you and what you think after reading this information if you want to take the risk or not. At least if you choose to move forward with this, you are well aware of what you are putting into your child, so God forbid if anything goes wrong, you fully understand why. Maybe with this knowledge, there will be fewer children with cancer by the age of two and any other diseases that are caused by poison. More information on chiropractic practice follows the vaccine information. I have posted the vaccine chart on my website as well for your convenience at www.mommysknowledge.com.

Vaccine Excipient & Media Summary
Excipients Included in U.S. Vaccines, by Vaccine

This table includes not only vaccine ingredients (e.g., adjuvants and preservatives), but also substances used during the manufacturing process, including vaccine-production media, that are removed from the final product and present only in trace quantities. In addition to the substances listed, most vaccines contain Sodium Chloride (table salt).

Last Updated September 2013

All reasonable efforts have been made to ensure the accuracy of this information, but manufacturers may change product contents before that information is reflected here. If in doubt, check the manufacturer's package insert.

Vaccine	Contains	Source: Manufacturer P.I. Dated
Adenovirus	sucrose, D-mannose, D-fructose, dextrose, potassium phosphate, plasdone C, anhydrous lactose, micro crystalline cellulose, polacrilin potassium, magnesium stearate, cellulose acetate phthalate, alcohol, acetone, castor oil, FD&C Yellow #6 aluminum lake dye, human serum albumin, fetal bovine serum, sodium bicarbonate, human-diploid fibroblast cell cultures (WI-38), Dulbecco's Modified Eagle's Medium, monosodium glutamate	March, 2011
Anthrax (Biothrax)	aluminum hydroxide, benzethonium chloride, formaldehyde, amino acids, vitamins, inorganic salts and sugars	May, 2012
BCG (Tice)	glycerin, asparagine, citric acid, potassium phosphate, magnesium sulfate, Iron ammonium citrate, lactose	February, 2009

DT (Sanofi)	aluminum potassium sulfate, peptone, bovine extract, formaldehyde, thimerosal (trace), modified Mueller and Miller medium, ammonium sulfate	December, 2005
DTaP (Daptacel)	aluminum phosphate, formaldehyde, glutaraldehyde, 2-Phenoxyethanol, Stainer-Scholte medium, modified Mueller's growth medium, modified Mueller-Miller casamino acid medium (without beef heart infusion), dimethyl 1-beta-cyclodextrin, ammonium sulfate	July, 2012
DTaP (Infanrix)	formaldehyde, glutaraldehyde, aluminum hydroxide, polysorbate 80, Fenton medium (containing bovine extract), modified Latham medium (derived from bovine casein), modified Stainer-Scholte liquid medium	July, 2012
DTaP-IPV (Kinrix)	formaldehyde, glutaraldehyde, aluminum hydroxide, Vero (monkey kidney) cells, calf serum, lactalbumin hydrolysate, polysorbate 80, neomycin sulfate, polymyxin B, Fenton medium (containing bovine extract), modified Latham medium (derived from bovine casein), modified Stainer-Scholte liquid medium	July, 2012

DTaP-HepB-IPV (Pediarix)	formaldehyde, gluteraldehyde, aluminum hydroxide, aluminum phosphate, lactalbumin hydrolysate, polysorbate 80, neomycin sulfate, polymyxin B, yeast protein, calf serum, Fenton medium (containing bovine extract), modified Latham medium (derived from bovine casein), modified Stainer-Scholte liquid medium, Vero (monkey kidney) cells	August, 2012
DTaP-IPV/Hib (Pentacel)	aluminum phosphate, polysorbate 80, formaldehyde, gutaraldehyde, bovine serum albumin, 2-phenoxethanol, neomycin, polymyxin B sulfate, Mueller's Growth Medium, Mueller-Miller casamino acid medium (without beef heart infusion), Stainer-Scholte medium (modified by the addition of casamino acids and dimethyl-beta-cyclodextrin), MRC-5 (human diploid) cells, CMRL 1969 medium (supplemented with calf serum), ammonium sulfate, and medium 199	July, 2012
Hib (ActHIB)	ammonium sulfate, formalin, sucrose, Modified Mueller and Miller medium	November, 2012
Hib (Hiberix)	formaldehyde, lactose, semi-synthetic medium	March, 2012
Hib (PedvaxHIB)	aluminum hydroxphosphate sulfate, ethanol, enzymes, phenol, detergent, complex fermentation medium	December, 2010

Hib/Hep B (Comvax)	yeast (vaccine contains no detectable yeast DNA), nicotinamide adenine dinucleotide, hemin chloride, soy peptone, dextrose, mineral salts, amino acids, formaldehyde, potassium aluminum sulfate, amorphous aluminum hydroxyphosphate sulfate, sodium borate, phenol, ethanol, enzymes, detergent	December, 2010
Hib/Mening. CY (MenHibrix)	tris (trometamol)-HCl, sucrose, formaldehyde, synthetic medium, semisynthetic medium	2012
Hep A (Havrix)	aluminum hydroxide, amino acid supplement, polysorbate 20, formalin, neomycin sulfate, MRC-5 cellular proteins	June, 2013
Hep A (Vaqta)	amorphous aluminum hydroxyphosphate sulfate, bovine albumin, formaldehyde, neomycin, sodium borate, MRC-5 (human diploid) cells	November, 2012
Hep B (Engerix-B)	aluminum hydroxide, yeast protein, phosphate buffers	July, 2012
Hep B (Recombivax)	yeast protein, soy peptone, dextrose, amino acids, mineral salts, potassium aluminum sulfate, amorphous aluminum hydroxyphosphate sulfate, formaldehyde, phosphate buffer	July, 2011
Hep A/Hep B (Twinrix)	formalin, yeast protein, aluminum phosphate, aluminum hydroxide, amino acids, phosphate buffer, polysorbate 20, neomycin sulfate, MRC-5 human diploid cells	August, 2012

Human Papillomavirus (HPV) (Cerverix)	vitamins, amino acids, lipids, mineral salts, aluminum hydroxide, sodium dihydrogen phosphate dehydrate, 3-O-desacyl-4' Monophosphoryl lipid A, insect cell, bacterial, and viral protein.	August, 2012
Human Papillomavirus (HPV) (Gardasil)	yeast protein, vitamins, amino acids, mineral salts, carbohydrates, amorphous aluminum hydroxyphosphate sulfate, L-histidine, polysorbate 80, sodium borate	March, 2013
Influenza (Afluria)	beta-propiolactone, thimerosol (multi-dose vials only), monobasic sodium phosphate, dibasic sodium phosphate, monobasic potassium phosphate, potassium chloride, calcium chloride, sodium taurodeoxycholate, neomycin sulfate, polymyxin B, egg protein, sucrose	April, 2013
Influenza (Agriflu)	egg proteins, formaldehyde, polysorbate 80, cetyltrimethylammonium bromide, neomycin sulfate, kanamycin	June, 2012
Influenza (Fluarix)	octoxynol-10 (Triton X-100), α-tocopheryl hydrogen succinate, polysorbate 80 (Tween 80), hydrocortisone, gentamicin sulfate, ovalbumin, formaldehyde, sodium deoxycholate, sucrose, phosphate buffer	May, 2013

Influenza (Flublok)	monobasic sodium phosphate, dibasic sodium phosphate, polysorbate 20, baculovirus and host cell proteins, baculovirus and cellular DNA, Triton X-100, lipids, vitamins, amino acids, mineral salts	December, 2012
Influenza (Flucelvax)	Madin Darby Canine Kidney (MDCK) cell protein, MDCK cell DNA, polysorbate 80, cetyltrimethlyammonium bromide, β-propiolactone, phosphate buffer	October, 2012
Influenza (Fluvirin)	nonylphenol ethoxylate, thimerosal (multidose vial– trace only in prefilled syringe), polymyxin, neomycin, beta-propiolactone, egg proteins, phosphate buffer	January, 2012
Influenza (Flulaval)	thimerosal, formaldehyde, sodium deoxycholate, egg proteins	February, 2013
Influenza (Fluzone: Standard, High-Dose, & Intradermal)	formaldehyde, octylphenol ethoxylate (Triton X-100), gelatin (standard trivalent formulation only), thimerosal (multi-dose vial only), egg protein, phosphate buffers, sucrose	April, 2013
Influenza (FluMist)	ethylene diamine tetraacetic acid (EDTA), monosodium glutamate, hydrolyzed porcine gelatin, arginine, sucrose, dibasic potassium phosphate, monobasic potassium phosphate, gentamicin sulfate, egg protein	July, 2013
Japanese Encephalitis (Ixiaro)	aluminum hydroxide, Vero cells, protamine sulfate, formaldehyde, bovine serum albumin, sodium metabisulphite, sucrose	May, 2013

Meningococcal (MCV4Menactra)	formaldehyde, phosphate buffers, Mueller Hinton agar, Watson Scherp media, Modified Mueller and Miller medium, detergent, alcohol, ammonium sulfate	November, 2011
Meningococcal (MCV4Menveo)	formaldehyde, amino acids, yeast extract, Franz complete medium, CY medium	August, 2013
Meningococcal (MPSV4Menomune)	thimerosal (multi-dose vial only), lactose, Mueller Hinton casein agar, Watson Scherp media, detergent, alcohol	October, 2012
MMR (MMR-II)	Medium 199, Minimum Essential Medium, phosphate, recombinant human albumin, neomycin, sorbitol, hydrolyzed gelatin, chick embryo cell culture, WI-38 human diploid lung fibroblasts	December, 2010

MMRV (ProQuad)	sucrose, hydrolyzed gelatin, sorbitol, monosodium L-glutamate, sodium phosphate dibasic, human albumin, sodium bicarbonate, potassium phosphate monobasic, potassium chloride, potassium phosphate dibasic, neomycin, bovine calf serum, chick embryo cell culture, WI-38 human diploid lung fibroblasts, MRC-5 cells	August, 2011
Pneumococcal (PCV13 – Prevnar 13)	casamino acids, yeast, ammonium sulfate, Polysorbate 80, succinate buffer, aluminum phosphate, soy peptone broth	January, 2013
Pneumococcal (PPSV-23 – Pneumovax)	Phenol.	October, 2011

Polio (IPV – Ipol)	2-phenoxyethanol, formaldehyde, neomycin, streptomycin, polymyxin B, monkey kidney cells, Eagle MEM modified medium, calf serum protein, Medium 199	December, 2005
Rabies (Imovax)	Human albumin, neomycin sulfate, phenol red indicator, MRC-5 human diploid cells, beta-propriolactone	December, 2005

Rabies (RabAvert)	β-propiolactone, potassium glutamate, chicken protein, ovalbuminegg protein, neomycin, chlortetracycline, amphotericin B, human serum albumin, polygeline (processed bovine 14 gelatin), sodium EDTA, bovine serum	March, 2012
Rotavirus (RotaTeq)	sucrose, sodium citrate, sodium phosphate monobasic monohydrate, sodium hydroxide, polysorbate 80, cell culture media, fetal bovine serum, vero cells [DNA from porcine circoviruses (PCV) 1 and 2 has been detected in RotaTeq. PCV-1 and PCV-2 are not known to cause disease in humans.]	June, 2013
Rotavirus (Rotarix)	amino acids, dextran, sorbitol, sucrose, calcium carbonate, xanthan, Dulbecco's Modified Eagle Medium (DMEM) [Porcine circovirus type 1 (PCV-1) is present in Rotarix. PCV-1 is not known to cause disease in humans.]	September, 2012
Smallpox (Vaccinia – ACAM2000)	human serum albumin, mannitol, neomycin, glycerin, polymyxin B, phenol, Vero cells, HEPES	September, 2009

Td (Decavac)	aluminum potassium sulfate, peptone, formaldehyde, thimerosal, bovine muscle tissue (US sourced), Mueller and Miller medium, ammonium sulfate	March, 2011
Td (Tenivac)	aluminum phosphate, formaldehyde, modified Mueller-Miller casamino acid medium without beef heart infusion, ammonium sulfate	December, 2010

Td (Mass Biologics)	aluminum phosphate, formaldehyde, thimerosal (trace), ammonium phosphate, modified Mueller's media (containing bovine extracts)	February, 2011
Tdap (Adacel)	aluminum phosphate, formaldehyde, glutaraldehyde, 2-phenoxyethanol, ammonium sulfate, Stainer-Scholte medium, dimethyl-beta-cyclodextrin, modified Mueller's growth medium, Mueller-Miller casamino acid medium (without beef heart infusion)	April, 2013
Tdap (Boostrix)	formaldehyde, glutaraldehyde, aluminum hydroxide, polysorbate 80 (Tween 80), Latham medium derived from bovine casein, Fenton medium containing a bovine extract, Stainer-Scholte liquid medium	February, 2013
Typhoid (inactivated – Typhim Vi)	hexadecyltrimethylammonium bromide, phenol, polydimethylsiloxane, disodium phosphate, monosodium phosphate, semi-synthetic medium	December, 2005

Typhoid (oral – Ty21a)	yeast extract, casein, dextrose, galactose, sucrose, ascorbic acid, amino acids, lactose, magnesium stearate	August, 2006
Varicella (Varivax)	sucrose, phosphate, glutamate, gelatin, monosodium L-glutamate, sodium phosphate dibasic, potassium phosphate monobasic, potassium chloride, sodium phosphate monobasic, potassium chloride, EDTA, residual components of MRC-5 cells including DNA and protein, neomycin, fetal bovine serum, human diploid cell cultures (WI-38), embryonic guinea pig cell cultures, human embryonic lung cultures	December, 2012
Yellow Fever (YF-Vax)	sorbitol, gelatin, egg protein	January, 2010
Zoster (Shingles – Zostavax)	sucrose, hydrolyzed porcine gelatin, monosodium L-glutamate, sodium phosphate dibasic, potassium phosphate monobasic, neomycin, potassium chloride, residual components of MRC-5 cells including DNA and protein, bovine calf serum	June, 2011

A table listing vaccine excipients and media by excipient can be found in:

Grabenstein JD. ImmunoFacts: Vaccines and Immunologic Drugs – 2013 (38th revision). St Louis, MO: Wolters Kluwer Health, 2012.

* This list of vaccines was found directly off the internet at this website. Please verify yearly for updated versions of this list.

* *www.cdc.gov/vaccines/pubs/pinkbook/downloads/appendicesb/excipient-table-2.pdf*
* *This post was taken down during the making of this book, in my opinion because of the bad publicity of the ingredients. But you may find a similar copy posted in vaxtruth.org/2011/08vaccine-ingredients/ it is posted by Megan Pond*
* *This site also gives more information about vaccines and each ingredient what side effects it has on a person. Very valuable!*
* *Ingredients depend on which modification is used.*

II. GLOSSARY AND DETAILS FOR INGREDIENTS

Product	Possible Ingredients*
2-Phenoxyethanol	2-Phenoxyethanol is a glycol either used as a preservative in vaccines
Aluminum	Aluminum is used in vaccines as an adjuvant, which helps the vaccine work more quickly and more powerfully.
Bovine casein	A casein is a family of phosphoproteins commonly found in mammalian milk. 80% of the proteins in cow's milk are casein. Bovine serum Bovine "[s]erum is the centrifuged fluid component of either clotted or defibrinated whole blood. Bovine serum comes from blood taken from domestic cattle. Serum from other animals is also collected and processed but bovine serum is processed in the greatest volume." "Bovine serum is a by-product of the meat industry. Bovine blood may be taken at the time of slaughter, from adult cattle, calves, very young calves or (when cows that are slaughtered are subsequently found to be pregnant) from bovine fetuses. It is also obtained from what are called 'donor' animals, which give blood more than once. Blood is available from bovine fetuses only because a proportion of female animals that are slaughtered for meat for human consumption are found (often unexpectedly) to be pregnant. Blood is available from very young calves because calves, especially males from dairy breeds, are often slaughtered soon, but not necessarily immediately, after birth because raising them will not be economically beneficial. Older animals are, of course, slaughtered for meat. Only donor cattle are raised for the purpose of blood donation. Donor cattle are invariably kept in specialized, controlled herds. Blood is taken from these animals in a very similar way to that used for human blood donation.

	Irrespective of whether blood is taken at slaughter or from donors, the age of the animal is an important consideration because it impacts the characteristics of the serum. Bovine serum is categorized according to the age of the animal from which the blood was collected as follows: • 'Fetal bovine serum' comes from fetuses • 'Newborn calf serum' comes from calves less than three weeks old • 'Calf serum' comes from calves aged between three weeks and 12 months • 'Adult bovine serum' comes from cattle older than 12 months Serum processed from donor blood is termed 'donor bovine serum'. Donor animals can be up to three years old."
Chicken Eggs	Viruses can be grown in chicken eggs before being used in vaccinations.
CMRL-1969	L-alanine, L-arginine (free base)b, L-aspartic acid, L-cysteine-HCL, L-cystine, L-glutamic acid-H20, L-gluatamine, glycine, L-histidine (free base)b, L-hydroxyproline, L-isoleucine, L-leucine, L-lysine, L-methionine, L-phenylalanine, L-proline, L-serine, L-threonine, L-tryptophan, L-tyrosine, L-valine, p-amino benzoic acid, ascorbic acid, d-biotin, calcium pantothenate, cholesterol, choline chloride, ethanol, folic acid, glutathione, i-inositol, menadione, nicotinamide, nicotinic acid, pyridoxal-HCL, pyridoxine-HCL, riboflavin, riboflavine-5-phosphate, sodium acetate-3H2O, thiamine-HCL, Tween 80, vitamin A acetate, vitamin D (calciferol), vitamin E (a-tocopherol phosphate), D-glucose, phenol red, sodium chloride, potassium chloride, calcium chloride, magnesium culphate heptahydrate, sodium phosphate dibasic, sodium dihydrogen phosphate, monopotassium phosphate, sodium bicarbonate, iron nitrate nonahydrate

Dulbecco's Modified Eagle's Serum	glucose, sodium bicarbonate, L-glutamine, pyridoxine HCl, pyridocal HCl, folic acid, phenol red, HEPES (2-[4-(2-hydroxyethyl)piperazin-1-yl]ethane sulfonic acid), L-methionine, L-cystine, sodium phosphate mono-basic, sodium pyruvate, vitamins
Earle's Balanced Salt Medium	inorganic salts, D-glucose, phenol red, calcium, magnesium salts
Fenton Medium	bovine extract
Formaldehyde	Formaldehyde is used in vaccines to inactivate the virus so the person being inoculated does not contract the disease
Human albumin	Human albumin is a blood plasma protein produced in the liver that, among other functions, transports hormones, fatty acids, and other compounds, and buffers pH.
Insect Cells	Cabbage moth and fall armyworm cells are used to grown viruses for vaccines
Latham Medium	bovine casein
MDCK (Madin-Carby canine kidney cells)	cells from normal female adult Cocker Spaniel (harvested in 1958 by SH Madin and NB Darby), EMEM(EBSS) (Eagle's Minimum Essential Medium with Earle's Balanced Salt Solution), glutamine, non-essential amino acids, fetal bovine serum
Mouse Brains	Live mice brains are inoculated with the Japanese encephalitis virus to grow the virus used in the vaccine
MRC-5	Medical Research Council 5, human diploid cells (cells containing two sets of chromosomes) derived from the normal lung tissues of a 14-week-old male fetus aborted for "psychiatric reasons" in 1966 in the United Kingdom, Earle's Basal Medium in Earle's balanced salt solution with bovine serum.
Mueller Hinton Agar	beef extract, acid hydro sate of casein, starch, agar

Muller-Miller Medium	glucose, sodium chloride, sodium phosphate dibasic, monopotassium, phosphate, magnesium sulfate hydrate, ferrous sulfate heptaphydrate, cystine hydrochloride, tyrosine hydrochloride, uracil hydrochloride, Ca-pantothenate in ethanol, thiamine in ethanol, pyridoxine-hydrochloride in ethanol, riboflavin in ethanol, biotin in ethanol, sodium hydroxide, beef heart infusion (de-fatted beef heart and distilled water), casein solution
Polysorbate 80	Also called Tween 80, Alkest 80, or Canarcel 80 (brand names). Polysorbate 80 is used as an excipient (something to basically thicken a vaccine for proper dosing) and an emulsifier (something to bond the ingredients)
Porcine gelatin	Gelatin is used to protect viruses in vaccines from freeze-drying or heat and to stabilize vaccines so they stay stable
Stainer-Scholte Liquid Medium	tris hydrochloride, tris base, glutamate (monosodium salt), proline, salt, monopotassium phosphate, potassium chloride, magnesium chloride, calcium chloride, ferrous sulfate, ascorbic acid, niacin, glutathione
Thimerosal	Thimerosal is an organ mercury compound used as a preservative
Vero Cells (African Green Monkey Cells)	cells derived from the kidney of a normal, adult African Green monkey in 1962 by Y. Yasumura and Y. Kawakita
WI-38 human diploid cells	Windstar Institute 38, human diploid lung fibroblasts derived from the lung tissues of a female fetus aborted because the family felt they had too many children in 1964 in the United States

Alternative Medicine to Vaccines

Other than natural remedies mentioned in this book and others you may come across, chiropractic practice helps the body align and help itself. All the nerves are put in place and help the immune system grow stronger; in return, the body grows stronger. A trained chiropractor can align and help cure individuals from birth and beyond. People are realizing this more and more each day and are starting their families early in life on this healthy way of living rather than drugs. Here are examples and information on chiropractic practice.

A note from Dr. Eddy Martinez (Chiropractic Practice)

LIFETIME FAMILY WELLNESS

To make the dream of a subluxation-free world a reality, Coconut Grove Chiropractic must educate the public about the importance of lifetime wellness care for all members of the family. In the past people believed that because they didn't have any obvious symptoms of a disease they were leading full, healthy lives. Today, we must understand that being healthy goes far beyond an absence of acute or chronic illness. Today, we know the health means performing at the peak of our potential physically, emotionally, and chemically.

A subluxation is when a bone in the spine slips out of place and blocks messages being released both to and from the brain. The result is chaos among cells and organs unable to organize and function to their fullest potential.

The word sub-lux-ation, when broken down, means less than 100% light to your internal environment (nation). Without light there is death. That is why we call subluxation the "Silent Killer".

PAIN IS NOT THE PROBLEM

A young couple was in getting checked for subluxation and they asked me when they could expect the pain and stiffness from their new exercise program to stop. My response was if you don't hurt after exercise you haven't trained. The general principle of weight training is that by lifting the weight you tear muscle fibers. This creates an inflammation in the muscle. As the muscle repairs itself it rebuilds itself bigger. The take away here is that the mission of innate intelligence is to adapt us to our world.

The stress of the exercise incites an innate adaptive and healing response, which, even though painful, makes us stronger. If you were to take a drug to shut this adaptive response off you would be cheating yourself out of what you are trying to create. Remember you have an infinite potential within in you, your innate intelligence. It is capable of adapting you to anything life throws at you. If it is flowing over your nervous system without interference the by product is maximum adaptability, maximum health potential, maximum expression of *your* potential, from within out. Physical, chemical and emotional stressors are always challenging us. If they overwhelm our adaptive capacity we sub luxate. The subluxation then dims down the expression of this intelligence.

Chiropractors analyze people for the presence of subluxation and remove it through the adjustment, thereby restoring the optimum flow of this wisdom. This magnificent inner wisdom doesn't need any help, just no interference. Simple? Absolutely! Powerful beyond measure?

Incredibly so! Live fully connected to your innate for your lifetime with regular chiropractic care. **Dr. Eddie Martinez DC**

CHIROPRACTIC AND THE IMMUNE SYSTEM

Ronald Pero, Ph.D., chief of cancer prevention research at New York's Preventive Medicine Institute and professor of medicine at New York University, performed one of the most important studies showing the positive effect chiropractic care can have on the immune system and general health. Dr. Pero measured the immune systems of people under chiropractic care as compared to those in the general population and those with cancer and other serious diseases. In his initial three-year study of 107 individuals who had been under chiropractic care for five years or more, the chiropractic patients were found to have a 200% greater immune competence than people who had not received chiropractic care, and 400% greater immune competence than people with cancer and other serious diseases.

The immune system superiority of those under chiropractic care did not diminish with age. Dr. Pero stated: When applied in a clinical framework, I have never seen a group other than this chiropractic group to experience a 200% increase over the normal patient s. This is why it is so dramatically important. We have never seen such a positive improvement in a group.

Pero R. "Medical Researcher Excited By CBSRF Project Results. " The Chiropractic Journal, August 1989; 32.

The chiropractic immunology connection was strengthened in 1991 when Patricia Brennan, Ph.D. and other researchers conducted a study that found improved immune response following chiropractic treatment. Specifically, the study demonstrated the phagocytic respiratory burst of polymorph nuclear neutrophils (PMN) and monocytes were enhanced in adults that had been adjusted by chiropractors. In other words, the cells that act like "Pac-Man" eating and destroying bad cells are enhanced through chiropractic care.

Brennan P, Graham M, Triano J, Hondras M. "Enhanced phagocytic cell respiratory bursts induced by spinal manipulation: Potent ial Role of Substance P." J Manip Physiolog Ther 1991; (14) 7:399-400.

Another important study was performed at the Sid E. Williams Research Center of Life Chiropractic University. The researchers took a group of HIV positive patient s and adjusted them over a six-month period. What they found was that the patients that were adjusted had an increase of forty-eight percent (48%) in the CD4 cells (an important immune system component). These measurements were taken at the patients' independent medical center, where they were under medical supervision for the condition. The control group (the patients that were not adjusted) did not demonstrate this dramatic increase in immune function, but actually experienced a 7.96% decrease in CD4 cell counts over the same period.

When we read the results of that study we were shocked that we hadn't heard about it earlier, which it didn't make the headline news or was on the front page of every newspaper. Those are very impressive results with important implications!

Selano JL, Hightower BC, Pfleger B, Feeley-Collins K, Grostic JD. "The Effects of Specific Upper Cervical Adjustments on the CD4 Counts of HIV Positive Patients." The Chiro Research Journal; 3(1); 1994.

This information was given to us by Dr. Eddy Martinez for the use of this book to inform people about alternatives to health care.

The Second Half of Baby's First Year

Your baby is now becoming more independent; he or she is learning how to roll over, sit up, crawl, stand, cruise (walk while holding on), and walk alone. This is a very exciting time for all of you, especially for the babies because they discover they can be independent. It becomes their new favorite thing! Though this is great for all of you and less stress on Mommy's body, it also means more stress from watching out for your baby and being quick on your toes. Put your running shoes on and baby-proof the house. We don't want our favorite little person getting hurt more than he or she has to.

It comes to my attention that moms are finding out that their babies' temper tantrums do not start at two years old. Oh no! They start around the eight- to nine-month-old mark. These, of course, are not exactly like the tantrums they have at two years old, because those are intentional. These tantrums occur because your baby is now trying to express emotions, now that he or she is more aware of life and what he or she wants, as well as a desire for independence and the frustrations caused by limitations.

But breathe! These tantrums really only last about ninety seconds or so before the child gets over it or is distracted by something else. Even if the baby falls and gets hurt, unless it is a major deal and he or she needs medical attention, the cry will usually last about ninety seconds. Just calm your baby in your arms; if the crying is bad to the point that he or she stops breathing for more than three to four seconds, just blow a little bit of air in his or her face and tap his or her back like a stern burp, and your baby will automatically breathe again. After the ninety seconds, all will be okay!

As your baby gets older, knows more, and is aware of things, the frustrating part becomes communicating those emotions and being independent as he or she figures out his or her new body and deals with limitations compared to the knowledge he or she has acquired— hence the tantrums. The baby just needs to be comforted and geared in a direction that he or she can handle. You could also give him or her a little help doing the task at hand. Talk to your baby, I mean all the time. Even if you feel stupid talk them through the day, what you are doing, even if you are not facing your baby let him or her know what you are doing step by step. For example when you are dressing your baby or changing his or her diaper, or even cooking dinner, playing, bathing, walking anything really. This will build up vocabulary words in his or her head and soon your baby will understand the task and follow some instructions as well as try to repeat what you say.

By this time, you will be able to enjoy your baby a lot more as far as fun activities. If your baby may say a few words by this time, at about ten to twelve months, then you can have a small dialogue, which is refreshing after spending a year talking to your baby without getting a response. Trust me you will be able to figure out what your baby is saying even if it is not perfect or clear in your language. Some babies take longer to develop especially if they are learning more than one language at a time so please do not be discouraged if your baby is not talking by the age of one. Remember boys usually take longer developing motor skills than girls. Generally.

Motherhood is finally growing on you, and you are more comfortable in your own skin, knowing your baby and doing what your baby needs and wants. The feeling of confidence is now in your blood, which is also refreshing after not knowing what to do when your little one first arrived. Now you get to play and have fun while teaching your baby his or her first essential steps to becoming an independent person. Yay!

You deserve a party! You did it! You made it through your first year with your baby. You have done a great job! Your baby is alive, happy, and healthy. Your husband is alive. I hope you made it through your first year with a healthy marriage and are not in line for divorce. Most important, you are in one piece and are able to keep going and take care of your family. If you're a single mom or dad, you deserve a medal! You did it all on your own. It was absolutely *not* easy, but you overcame every obstacle and did it great! You rock! We all rock!

Your baby will be turning one now, and when you look back, you wonder, *Where did the time go?* Yeah, there went your baby; now look at your child and enjoy him or her. The first birthday is a time when you need to celebrate all these things, all your accomplishments through the roughest year, not only because you have met all of the changes and challenges to you as a mom and your new baby in a new world with all its discoveries, but also because you have accomplished huge hurtles. If you are married, you've gotten to really know yourself and your partner more than you ever did; the connection and new life that you and your partner had to endure, the strains and happiness this blessing of a child has brought to your life, embracing the joy and sadness as well as the gifts each child brings with him or her to you and your family. Most of all, you have succeeded in getting to know who you have become as a person, a partner, and as a parent.

This party is not only celebrating your baby's first year of life but also all that has happened with your life too. Party on and make it how you want it, because you may never get that chance again. From here on out, it's what your child wants for his or her birthday. Well, maybe you'll get lucky and get to choose the second birthday too. Congratulations!

Month's Ahead

For the months ahead when your baby is about one and a half or so up to two years old, which is when the big tantrums that deserve discipline start. The tantrums soften out until about four years of age and then start again. So be aware, be prepared, know what stage you are in, and just breathe! You are not a bad mother if your baby does cry, even if it's in public. If you need to cry too because of frustration or the incident hurt you too, then go ahead. It's okay!

Potty training is another hurdle you may start to tackle once your child starts to show signs usually between eighteen to twenty months. The first signs are interest in the potty, hiding to poop and being uncomfortable in a dirty diaper. If you try too early your child may regress and want to be in diapers a lot longer than they have too. *Welcome to the toddler years!*

I hope this book has helped you through your pregnancy and first year of parenthood. I just hope it has made your journey a little bit easier with these tips and the explanation of emotional differences of motherhood.

Research Sources

- Parenting information, vaccine and health information and other related information and articles found in ***authors website***: *www.mommysknowledge.com*
- *The Happiest Baby on the Block* Book and Video information by: **Harvey Karp, M.D.**
- Allergy information on nutrition found at *www.safbaby.com*
- Vaccine information and other health related sources and news are found at *www.thegreatergood.org*
- Chart of a table listing vaccine excipients and media by excipient can be found in: *Grabenstein JD. ImmunoFacts: Vaccines and Immunologic Drugs – 2013 (38th revision). St Louis, MO: Wolters Kluwer Health, 2012.*
- This list of vaccines was found directly off the internet at this website. *www.cdc.gov/vaccines/pubs/pinkbook/downloads/appendicesb/excipient-table-2.pdf* Another site available with this information is *www.vaxtruth.org/2011/08vaccine-ingredients/* **written by Megan Pond.**
- Alternative Medicine Information provided by: **Dr. Eddy Martinez (Chiropractic Practice)** and his sources:
  - *Pero R. "Medical Researcher Excited By CBSRF Project Results. " The Chiropractic Journal, August 1989; 32.*
  - *Brennan P, Graham M, Triano J, Hondras M. "Enhanced phagocytic cell respiratory bursts induced by spinal manipulation: Potent ial Role of Substance P." J Manip Physiolog Ther 1991; (14) 7:399-400.*
  - *Selano JL, Hightower BC, Pf leger B, Feeley-Collins K, Grostic JD. "The Effects of Specific Upper Cervical Adjustments on the CD4 Counts of HIV Positive Patients." The Chiro Research Journal; 3(1); 1994.*

About the Author

Krizia earned an associate degree in journalism, but she has always been writing something throughout her life. Whether it was a song or a poem, she has always had something to say and a strong, practical opinion on things that really mattered most to her. Now as a mother, Krizia found herself at a point in her life when everything she knew had changed.

In the last semester of her master's in art, Krizia stopped teaching to finish her degree. The news of a baby took her life by storm and sent her in a new direction completely. Going from being a fast-paced, independent woman with a goal in her life to a dependent, engaged woman finishing up school with no chance to work once she graduated took a big toll on her plans. She knew one thing for sure: that her life was going to change drastically.

She was the first of her friends to have a child, so no one really took her under her wing to help much. Just a few tips here and there from family were all she knew. Reading a lot of baby books while pregnant, she found that none of them prepared her for the psychological changes of pregnancy and parenthood. This made her want to write a book based on the psychological aspect of pregnancy and parenthood to help people with the hard first year a parent actually goes through, hoping to touch other parents' lives and make this process a lot easier. The book focuses on the subjects that most people do not want to talk about: the truth about life and being a parent-to-be and a new parent.

About the Book

This book describes some of the psychological and physical aspects of pregnancy and parenthood that the other books about what to expect missed out on. I am writing to the women who have gotten pregnant unplanned, have been raped, or find themselves as teen moms—or in any other circumstances, even planned pregnancies. This book has helpful tips on parenting, maintaining your health, and dealing with issues encountered during pregnancy and parenting for the entire family. It covers the psychological aspect of what is okay to feel or not to feel during pregnancy and parenthood, the realization of loss of oneself as a person, and what to expect and deal with the first year of parenthood. There are also helpful tips for dads to understand what the mom is going through as well as guidelines to have a functioning household once the baby arrives, including what you really need for the baby and the hospital, how much babies cost, and vaccination and alternative medicines. More information on this and other important parenting matters is available on the author's blog at *www.mommysknowledge.com.*